MW00805916

Funk to

Fabulous

In 14 Days

A Neuropsychologist's Brain Hacks
to Stop Worrying
&
Boost Happiness

Mary C. Wetherby, Ph.D.

Mind Candy Publishing

Copyright © 2024 by Dr. Mary M. C. Wetherby

All rights reserved.

No portion of this book may be reproduced in any form without written permission from the publisher or author, except as permitted by U.S. copyright law.

Book Cover by Eddie Roseboom

Disclaimer

Hey there, dear reader! Welcome to this fascinating book filled with informational and educational nuggets! But hold up, before we dive in, let's set some ground rules for a joyful reading experience:

- First things first, this book is all about fun learning, not a substitute for therapy or treatment. So, nope, it won't cure your fear of clowns or your sudden craving for cheese puffs.

- Dr. Wetherby may be a doctor, but she's not your personal doc. Remember, this is more like a friendly chat over a cup of hot cocoa.

- While we're eager to share ideas and suggestions, they aren't a replacement for professional guidance. If you need advice, consult your trusted mental health pro or physician.

- Neither the publisher nor the author should be held responsible if you suddenly decide to take up tightrope walking or try out extreme knitting after reading this book. Just saying!

- Oh, and no guarantees about life-changing outcomes here. We're not fortune-tellers, but we sure hope you'll gain some valuable insights and have a blast!

- If you find yourself in a pickle and need immediate assistance, remember, call your local emergency number or mental health crisis hotline for some genuine superhero help.

Now that we've got that out of the way, let's embark on a thrilling journey of knowledge and giggles! Happy reading!

Contents

For Kev, who has been there with me every step of the way, even when those steps required a heap of positivity and even more humor.

For my mom Martha Bottom Cubbedge, who taught me to "Climb Every Mountain."

Preface

Happiness is one of life's greatest pursuits. Even if you have been beaten up by life, happiness can happen. Struggles do not have to define you. Throughout my years of practice as a neuropsychologist, I have discovered that there tend to be common elements that help people attain happiness. So, I developed strategies that I find help person after person get closer to their goal of happiness, regardless of the other issues the person is facing. These strategies are like tools for your tool belt, ready to be pulled out and used for a tune-up at any time that they are needed.

People tend to hold onto "sameness" to give them a sense of control and coping. Living with sameness and without change is not happiness. It is a desperate attempt at band-aiding together an illusion of coping with daily existence. Generally, for people to tolerate change, it must come slowly. Gradual change allows folks to go through the process of fighting the change, yet ultimately adapting little by little.

As people began experiencing pandemic life of 2020, change happened quickly. The onset of the pandemic was not the gradual change that people tend to cope with better. Because the change to life was so sudden, and reality became different so quickly, the coping skills that many people had cobbled together to manage daily life fell by the wayside. There was no more structure and routine to help offset mood and anxiety snags. Folks could not run to the movies to distract themselves from a mood funk. Social networks from work and school fell apart. Play dates, outings for lunches, game nights, fundraisers, and in-person hang out sessions were no more. Rituals to support and grieve loved ones were stripped away. Supply chain problems meant that the same stuff in the same quantities was not available. Isolation set in.

Even if you are not experiencing sudden changes in your life, there are always other life issues coming at you that can threaten your coping and happiness. Today, through technology, we are more connected than ever. One would think that having this access would help with coping. However, in many ways, folks are more isolated. Technology may have improved our lives in some ways, but it has made us no closer to happiness. It is difficult to take a day off from work or school when Wi-Fi is available. Students and adults alike are so pushed toward higher-level goals and achievements, that the importance of happiness is devalued. There is more looking at outward achievements rather than inward success.

Typically, when we look for happiness, we erroneously search for complicated solutions. Yet often, it is the simplest of things that bring happiness. My husband Kevin worked with people who lived in the dumps of Mexico. They washed and resold discarded bottles for their living. This group's poverty was so great that many of their children had developmental delays due to lack of nutrition. Yet, they were some of the most joyful people that my husband had ever met. He learned the greatest lesson from these people. Their happiness did not hinge on their circumstance, but rather came from their inner selves.

We have all had obstacles in life and challenges that are not easy. However, we can be happy with an imperfect life. I was in serious classical ballet training when I developed Juvenile Rheumatoid Arthritis at age twelve. Within three weeks, I went from athletic to not being able to get up from a chair. I am always in pain, and have so many joint replacements that I consider myself a cyborg! Similarly, my patients have physical, cognitive, or emotional struggles. But there can be joy in an imperfect life. Looking inward is the key.

After having pursued higher education for thirteen years post high school and practiced neuropsychology for over thirty years, I have worked with many different types of people. As a neuropsychologist, I have training in psychology as well as in brain function and how to diagnose cognitive disorders, including ADHD, memory, and learning disorders. I have evaluated and treated patients with brain injury, stroke, and chronic illness while working as Director of Neuropsychology on a Brain Injury Unit in a rehabilitation hospital. I have testified as a forensic expert on murder cases, treated patients at a trauma unit, and treated and consulted in regard to Alzheimer's and other dementia cases. I have also diagnosed and worked with people with autism to folks whose relationship was in shambles. What I have learned from all of my patients is this: No matter the situation, the one driving common element is the search for happiness.

While it is true that not everyone is going to be happy at all times, there can be a certain modus operandi for leading a generally happy life. As a neuropsychologist, I also have a unique perspective about how the brain is involved in our happiness. *Funk to Fabulous in 14 Days* was written in order to share the tools that I have developed over the years to help my patients reach their goal of happiness. These strategies were created to help people attain their happiness potential, which indeed should be considered "fabulousness!"

When we are talking about being happy, I refuse to be stuffy. The overarching message of my theory of psychology, Street Psychology, is "if it's not useful, it's useless." My goal with *Funk to Fabulous* is to deliver smart and helpful material, in a manner that is useable and not dreadfully boring. An added bonus is that you can go to **Funktofabulous.com** for additional funk to fabulous material. It's all about using your tools and staying on track, whatever works best for you!

So, enjoy *Funk to Fabulous* and have a big time going from funk to fabulous in fourteen days!

It's time to Rock and Roll into:

Tips to Ignite Your Spark

Scan the code below and I will email you free tips to ignite that inner spark!

DAY 1

Use the TOOLS

Use the TOOLS,

Oh Soon-To-Be FABULOUS One!!

Getting Happy

Happiness is not the absence of depression. Happiness is an activity in and of itself. But who wants to just be happy? I want you to be fabulous, darling! These tools are not only for those who have worries or anxiety, or battle depression, but also for those who just want to take their happiness up a notch!

As a neuropsychologist, I have developed strategies, or tools, for your beautiful brain to use. Once you have these tools in your cognitive tool belt, you can pull them out as needed, at any time in life. You can actually think your way to fabulous!

I'm giving you the tools for fabulous living. All you have to do is use them! Are you ready to get out of your day-to-day funk—fast?

If so, get ready to go from *Funk to Fabulous in 14 Days*!

And as an added bonus to help keep you on track is **Funktofabulous.com** where you'll find cool stuff to accompany you on your fabulous journey! And by popular demand, there is a *Funk to Fabulous* video course!

Let's Make A Deal

I'll make a deal with you. If you use the tools I describe in *Funk to Fabulous*, you can develop new ways to be happy and fabulous. The tools will help you reduce your funk, depression, worrying, and maybe even your anxiety. Depression and anxiety are often closely related. (You go over and over negative thoughts in your head, which makes you worried, leads to anxiety, and keeps you from being fabulous!) So improving one will naturally lead to improving the other.

What *Is* a FUNK?

A funk can be depression, or just "the blues." You can feel down-in-the-dumpolas or just plain blah. You could be jittery or nervous. It could just be a rut that you are in that is not fabulous, but is definitely not where you want to be. But what do you do about it?

We all feel like it's possible to be happier. Unfortunately, it's sometimes difficult to know exactly what "happier" means. We know where we already are, emotionally, and though we may want to change, understanding how to do it—and what to do—is easier said than done. We know that we want to head in a different direction, but where is that direction … and how do we get there?

What Is FABULOUS?

Fabulousness is a sparkly energy of you-ness. This is where you want to be. It is you at your best. When you head in this direction and reach your fabulous destination, the day goes from gray to technicolor. You feel better, and your world looks better. Best of all, you smile more!

Funk to Fabulous TOOLS

Everyone wants to experience happiness. Because something crappy has happened to you, during your day or during your life, does not mean that you cannot be happy. Throughout my years of practice as a neuropsychologist, I developed strategies, or tools, that I found helped person after person learn to deal with their struggles and get closer to their goal of happiness. These tools are to be actually used by you. At the beginning of the program, you will be using the tools daily.

Following each explanation of a *Funk to Fabulous* concept, you will read about a tool that you can actually use to help change your way of thinking or being. You will know that it is a tool for you to use because you will see a cute little morph person holding a tool. This morph is the signal that you are about to learn a tool that will help reinforce the concept. Follow the directions attached to each tool, and you will be on your way to fabulousness.

Whatever you do, don't forget about your cute little morph holding the tool! This is your visual cue that it is time to start applying the fun. Just think, "Morph after morph, tool after tool, more and more fabulous!" So start using the tools and building your new fabulous self!

Release Your Inner Wild Child!

There's only one catch: You have to actually *use* the tools. Often, people with stressful, busy lives have limited energy. That's a huge part of the funk. So you have to summon your strength from within—your inner strength, which is ready to rock and roll! Release your Inner Wild Child to actually read, then use, the tools in this book and work toward success. The hardest (but best!) part will be the first step.

Just think "One day at a time," and collect your rewards. You will receive one letter for each section you complete, which will, in the end, spell F-U-N-K T-O F-A-B-U-L-O-U-S. At the end of fourteen days, when you have received fourteen letters and completely spelled "Funk to Fabulous," you will have completed each step of the program. The tools to be out of your funk and totally fabulous will be yours!

Now, you may be one of these overachieving types, and if so, you can complete the *Funk to Fabulous* program in half the time. Just learn enough tools to achieve two letters per day. However, for the program to work, you must truly internalize the tools. If you use them too quickly, the tools may not stick. I want you to remain fabulous, even after reading the book and following your intensive *Funk to Fabulous* program! So, no matter how quickly you complete the program, in seven or fourteen days, make sure that you keep using your *Funk to Fabulous* tools so that those changes stick!

Funk to Fabulous FUNBOOK

Your companion book to *Funk to Fabulous in 14 Days* is the *Funk to Fabulous FUNBOOK*. It contains all of the forms that accompany your Tools, or strategies, that are listed in each chapter of *Funk to Fabulous*. With the *FUNBOOK*, you can quickly access all things *you*; the pages that you need to record your thoughts and behaviors to keep up with being fabulous! You can easily grab a copy and make it all yours. And, you can go to **Funktofabulous.com** for *FUNBOOK* stuff as well as the video course. Whatever works for you!

Your Fourteen-Day Focus!

For the next fourteen days, you are mine, mine, all mine! Your focus is to go from funk to fabulous. DO NOT embark on a major lifestyle change like quitting smoking or dieting during these fourteen days. You don't even have to clean your house if you don't want (you can quote me on this). Trying to initiate another major life change while concentrating on tool usage will likely sabotage any efforts that you are making toward getting out of your funk. I need your energy and focus to help you become fabulous. The tools described in this book are your only mission for the next fourteen days ... other than feeding the dog, obviously. (And then there's feeding the family, getting dressed, working. You know, stuff like that.)

Day Four

You might notice that Day Four is a little longer than the other days. Why? The focus of Day Four is organizing worry, and in order to understand how to do that, there are several tools required. Also, it is important to *understand* the dynamics behind this worry organization. So, in order to get all of that information together in one place, Day Four needs to be a little longer than the other days. The really great news is that once you are finished with Day Four, the rest of the days feel like smooth sailing!

What Are You Waiting For? TOMORROW?

(Spoiler Alert! Tomorrow never comes. Don't act like you didn't already know that!)

DO NOT wait until you *feel like* using the tools. If you are in a funk, and wait until you feel like using these tools, you will never use them. When first picking up the tools, you will feel as if you are just "going through the motions." Don't panic—that's okay. It happens. Ignore yourself and your trepidations, and keep using the tools. If you were to wait until you were feeling less funk-like to use a tool, as in until *tomorrow*, you would never use the tool. So ... don't be a tool; *use* the tools!

START FILLING YOUR FABULOUS TOOL BELT!

Hold onto your tool belt! Here's your first tool!

Fab-Doodles Tool

Grab a piece of soap and write on your bathroom mirror: "FABULOUS in fourteen days—more FABULOUS each day!" You may wonder about the wisdom in this. But if you have ever tried to write a book (or even a research paper for school), you will find that it is easy to veer slightly, or significantly, off topic without one simple thing: Your thesis statement, written on a scrap of paper taped to your desk. You are forced to refer to it often, so you can get back on track as needed. This strategy helped me get my dissertation written. That, and not eating as a daily reminder that I needed money to buy food— and thus needed to finish my education!

Seeing "FABULOUS in fourteen days—more FABULOUS each day!" written on your mirror first thing in the morning will be the daily reminder you need about your new mission! Every morning, rewrite the message with one day less. On Day Two, then, you'll write "FABULOUS in thirteen days—I'm more FABULOUS each day!" and so on. Continue your countdown each day. On Day Fourteen, you will write, "I've gone from FUNK to FABULOUS!"

There are fourteen letters in F-U-N-K T-O F-A-B-U-L-O-U-S, which works out perfectly for your fourteen-day program of fabulous transformation. With each day that you complete on your journey to fabulousness, you get to write another letter on your mirror. Or, you can cut out the cute Fab-Doodle letters provided here in this book. Be adventurous! Be creative! Doodle! Write fabulously fancy letters! Whatever makes your toes tingle! Create your own "Fab-Doodles." And throw in some love notes to yourself! After Day One, you get to Fab-Doodle the letter "F." Write it in soap on your mirror, with colored chalk on a chalkboard, using markers on a big piece of paper, or with anything that you can see on a daily basis. After Day Two, Fab-Doodle the letter "U."

Now, I realize that after Day Two, you will have the letters FU on your mirror. You have to have a sense of humor about yourself!

Fab-Doodles Soap
Love Notes

FAB-DOODLES SOAP LOVE NOTES

"FABULOUS in fourteen days—more FABULOUS each day!"

Other Inspirational FAB-DOODLE LOVE NOTES:

"Stop it with your delicious self!"

"You look MARVELOUS!"

(Write some of your own Soap Love Notes to yourself on the next page!)

MY FAB-DOODLES SOAP LOVE NOTES TO ME:

_____

_____

_____

_____

_____

_____

Yay Me!

Fab-Doodles

Here are some Fab-Doodles you can use!

Funk Production

Folks who have a tendency to be in a funk, full of worry, or depressed tend to have a "Leave it to Beaver" image of how the rest of humanity goes about their business of day-to-day living. They tend to think that other people are happy all the time, and that they are the only ones who are not. Listen, it's normal to be happier some days than others. This is the ebb and flow of everyday life. It's okay to laugh, cry, and become angry, frustrated, or jealous. These are all normal human emotions. Not getting hung up on the negative emotions and ruminating about them is the trick.

When you ruminate, or stew about something, you go over and over and over the same thought in your brain. This produces the funk. Unfortunately, ruminating is like a runaway train: Once it gets started, it is very difficult to stop. To top of it all off, people who are chronic worriers tend to be *experts* at stewing. They get the grand prize for being in a FUNK! (Don't be jealous, though—you'll get your FABULOUS award at the end of all of this. After all, being FABULOUS is an award in and of itself!) These folks have a significant amount of practice at staying in a funk, instead of practice becoming fabulous. But remember that it doesn't have to be that way—you don't have to let yourself get down in the dumps over every little thing. On the other hand, it's okay to worry a little bit, as long as you're worrying *correctly*. (The tools for which we will review later.) It's okay to not be deliriously happy ALL of the time. Don't panic when you're not having a good moment. If you do, then your funk will increase, and you will be less likely to use your tools. If you're not doing well, set down all of the negative self-talk in which you usually engage, and move forward by using the tools in this book.

I have worked with folks who use their tools, begin to feel better, and then stop using the tools *because* they feel better. For example, I may assign someone "worry time" (described later in the book, promise!) to help them stop worrying about upcoming travel plans, a painful memory, or a relationship problem with a parent or significant other. The next week, the funk has usually been alleviated. But then a few weeks later, that person has gone right back to worrying over every little thing!

Instead of continuing to use the "worry time," the person has returned to poor worry habits. Stress, hopelessness and lethargy are more severe. And of course, negative self-talk has run rampant. When folks feel like this it's even more important to remember that they *did* feel better when they used their tools!

In other words, instead of letting your funk get the best of you, beating yourself up, and saying to yourself that you will never feel better, you need to regroup and use the tools which will benefit you. If you stop using the tools and feel worse, pick them up again! They're not that heavy!

Funk Production Tool

So we know now that we have to stop the cycle of negativity if we're going to move forward, right? But how do we do that? We have to start from the bottom—with the negativity. One of the best ways to stop saying funk-producing bad things to yourself is to *replace* those negative statements with positive ones. Write down three solid positive things about yourself, to which you can refer when you notice that you are beating yourself up with funk-producing statements. It is important to write these positive statements down ahead of time, before you are in a particularly poor mood. If you wait until you are in a funk to produce those three solid positive statements about yourself, it is much more difficult to come up with sparkly, optimistic, and affirmative thoughts. So come up with some now (you can always add more later)! You can even use the ones provided here!

I will help you get started:

- I can be successful.

- I am a beautiful person.

- I am doing well for the life I have lived, but that is not working for me anymore, so I am making a positive change.

- I am loved.

- I have good friends.

- I have the rest of my life ahead of me.

- I can enjoy the moment.

- I have the ability to make changes if I want to.

When you notice that you are having a negative thought about yourself, pull out your list! Identify the negative conversations in your brain that you are having about yourself and REPLACE those thoughts with positive ones!

Fabulous Me Form

FABULOUS

ME!

Your turn:

I **AM** _____.

I am _____.

I am _____.

I am _____.

I am _____.

I am _____.

I **CAN** _____.

I can _____.

I can _____.

I can _____.

I can _____.

I can _____.

Medical Aspects of the Funk

This book focuses on going from Funk to Fabulous without the use of medication. Many people who use *Funk to Fabulous* simply want to be happier and more fabulous. Some people may have depression and/or anxiety, and use the *Funk to Fabulous* tools to help. At times, one might have depression and/or anxiety that is so severe that some sort of medication therapy might be used. In those cases, the tools in this book can be used in conjunction with medication. Outcomes in such situations tend to be best when a person is not only taking medication, but also using non-medication therapies. The tools in this book can be used to help with medication if you must take it, or as stand-alone tools. Either way, the tools can help with the funk!

If you feel you are experiencing significant depression and/or anxiety, a good physical may be in order. There are medical issues that can contribute to mood problems, like thyroid dysfunction. Hormone level issues, either chronic or cyclical, can add to mood fluctuations and depression. Mood problems may also occur with heart disease, bypass surgery, stroke, and more.

You may even be taking medication that contributes to depression. Tranquilizers can increase mood problems in some people, as can pain medication, steroids, and other medications. There are multiple other problems that can give rise to mood issues, like addiction, too much alcohol, and the use of uncontrolled substances. Overall, it's a good idea to cover all your bases by consulting with your physician if need be.

The focus of this book is to propel you from funk to fabulous. Getting depression and/or anxiety diagnosed, if you have it, and having other problems like medical issues ruled out, is a necessary step. And you can still use this book to help you become fabulous!

If you are using this book to help increase your happiness and fabulousness, and you do not have serious mood problems, that's great! Let's get tool belting!

Medical Aspects of the Funk Tool

Pick up the phone, call your doctor, and get some tests run if it's necessary. Make sure that you are in tip-top shape. If you are in a funk, you may find that you want to put off calling and making an appointment. Don't stall! Do it now. You can still jump into using the tools in this book while you're waiting for your appointment!

My appointment is on:

_____

With:

_____

Also, realize that other issues may contribute toward your funk, like some of the problems we just discussed. These may include some medical problems or medications. Consult your physician about medications or treatments you may be taking that can contribute to a funk. It's important that you know about any barriers to fabulousness!

Medications I want to ask my physician about include:

_____

_____

_____

_____

If you do find that you have medical issues which are adding to the funk, address them! If you discover that some of your medications might be making you depressed, ask your doctor if there are alternatives. In the meantime, you can still work on training your brain to be more fabulous with your new tools!

Other questions I have for my doctor about my health or mood:

_____

_____

_____

_____

Weird questions I've always wanted to ask my doctor:
(You're already there – might as well!)

_____

_____

_____

_____

Give Yourself an "F!"

CONGRATULATIONS!!!

You have completed DAY ONE!

Give yourself an

You're gonna dominate this!

Now dive into dynamite:

DAY 2

Don't "Try"

Be aware of roadblocks that you set up for yourself—and then get rid of them! Often, when I am explaining a new tool to a patient, that patient will respond with, "I'll try." This is one of my pet peeves. When people say that they will "try," they are already halfway committed to failing and staying in a funk. The "I'll try" thinking does not set up the expectation that you will succeed and be fabulous. The "I'll try" brain does not believe in itself.

People are afraid of changing behaviors. "New" is the unknown. It is the new "scared." People are more comfortable with dysfunctional behaviors than they are with change. If you are honest with yourself, you may find that you are comfortable with your funk. Hanging onto old behaviors is like wearing an old bathrobe that has holes in it. You like your old bathrobe because it's familiar to you. You know what to expect when you put it on. The problem is that it is not *functional*. It is not really keeping you warm anymore. But here comes the next big, scary step: You have to get rid of your old, worn-out bathrobe and get a new one that will actually function, and keep you warm. And you have to trust that the new bathrobe will help you be fabulous!

Sometimes I feel like I'm trying to wrench the old, disgusting bathrobe out of my patients' hands, while they're desperately hanging on. **People hold on to bad things due to fear of change.** Unfortunately, sometimes, bad things feel safe. But you will never know how much better the new bathrobe feels until you get rid of the old one and actually try the new one on. When people say, "I'll try," I know that they fear the positive change. They actually fear fabulousness. People feel the need to mollify themselves by saying that they are going to take a stab at the new behavior I am suggesting, even though they know down deep that they are not set on succeeding. They have not completely committed to being fabulous.

If you find that you are not using these new tools, you may be "stuck" in that same way. People get "stuck" when they fear change. They pull on the old bathrobe with holes in it and begin shivering, then wonder why. Being stuck is also like running around in circles, getting nowhere fast. Except also imagine that you're wearing an old and worn out bathrobe with holes in it while you're running in circles. Not a good look.

If you think you are stuck, and this is sounding familiar, ask yourself:

- "In what way am I benefitting from being stuck?"

- "Does being miserable feel familiar and safe?"

- "Does change for the better feel like too much of a risk?"

- "Would I actually rather stay in my funk than take a risk to be fabulous?"

The time for change is now. But you have to do something about it, because this is your life, and you're the one making the calls. If you feel that change isn't safe for you, and is like stepping out of an airplane, then let the tools in *Funk to Fabulous in 14 Days* be your parachute.

Don't Try Tool

Starting today, you'll have a new "un-habit." You will stop masking your fear of change by saying, "I'll try." It's OK if you're uncomfortable. It's OK if you're scared. Just try on the change and do it, whatever "it" is. When you find yourself saying, "I'll try," you need to realize that you have committed yourself to possibly failing. You are saying that the status quo funk is OK with you. By saying, "I'll try," you are saying that you are OK with not being fabulous and staying in a funk. TODAY, make a decision to use a new tool and make a change.

Do not say, "I'll try."

Say, "I WILL!"

Remember: Fabulousness Is an Active Sport!

Change It Form

I'll try to:

_____.

CHANGE IT

I will:

_____.

The thing that was keeping me STUCK:

_____.

- -

I'll try to:

_____.

CHANGE IT

I will:

_____.

The thing that was keeping me STUCK:

_____.

- -

I'll try to:

_____.

CHANGE IT

I will:

_____.

The thing that was keeping me STUCK:

_____.

- -

I'll try to:

_____.

CHANGE IT

I will:

_____.

The thing that was keeping me STUCK:

_____.

- -

Yes...But

Another problem that I often run across is when a patient begins "yes butting." You do *not* want to be a "yes butter."

Every time you look into your refrigerator to grab some butter, I want you to ask yourself, "Was I a *yes butter* today?"

Saying "yes but" usually occurs whenever a new behavior is suggested to a person. Sometimes, a patient will be frustrated with a problem he or she is having. If that patient is a "yes butter," no matter what I suggest, the response may very well be "yes . . . but."

A very clear instance of yes butting happens in regard to getting children to sleep in their own beds. Even though the parents may state that independent sleep is a therapy goal, I get "yes buts" from both parents and children at each suggested strategy. Having a child sleep in the bed with the parent may be endearing to the parent when that child is very young, but can cause problems for both the child and parent later on. In the tween and teen years, a child who is still sleeping in the parents' bed may have problems with sleepovers, and the parents may not be able to have their own room—or bed!—to themselves.

At the suggestion of a gradual transition to her own bed, I had one child respond, "*Yes* I could start lying in my own bed for fifteen minutes every night, *but* my father is sleeping in my room now." I then suggested that the father could go to sleep in her room *after* her fifteen-minute sleep exercise. She responded, "*Yes, but* my father goes to bed before me. I stay up later than him, so that won't work." When I then suggested that the father go to sleep initially in his own bed and then move to the child's room after the child's fifteen-minute sleep exercise, the mother responded, "Yes, but he needs his sleep and does not like to be awakened." I then asked if sleeping in her own bed was still a therapy goal for the child. When I was told yes, I mentioned that, given that the father seemed most enthusiastic about moving back to his own bed, he may be willing to sacrifice a little to help make this happen.

"Yes butting" often follows a pattern. As described above, there is usually agreement with an observation or suggestion I am making ("yes") and then a reason that the new tool or task cannot be initiated ("but"). That "yes butting" person is afraid of leaving his or her funk! The child and parent are likely gaining something by staying stuck in the old behavior, so they protect it by saying "yes but." The child may have doubts about her ability to survive independently from the parent. She may feel she gets more attention than her siblings if she sleeps with the parent, or gain attention from the parent by sleeping with her (as opposed to other, healthier ways of getting parental attention), or she may be dealing with anxiety by sleeping with the parent (as opposed to more adaptive ways of dealing with anxiety). The parent may be "yes butting" about the child sleeping independently because she wants to feel needed, fears her child's independence, or wants to avoid intimacy with her husband.

Sometimes patients say, "yes, but" when one of their negative thoughts that is keeping them stuck is pointed out. For example, I may say, "You are so ready to believe negative things about yourself, but absolutely refuse to believe anything good." The "yes butter" patient responds, "Yes, but the good things are not true."

The patient is refusing to process what I just said. She is trying to justify the reason to remain in a funk, because fabulousness is just too scary. She will not think to herself, "*What is it that makes me give more validity, and believe so much more readily, negative things about myself? What is wrong with believing the good things just as readily?*" She is instead immediately defending the current way that she is, with a "yes but," instead of considering change. Saying "yes, but" keeps you in a negative place, and ensures that you will remain miserable and in a funk.

Don't say, "Yes, but." Just say, "Yes."

Yes...But Tool

One of my favorite quotes comes from *Pee Wee's Big Adventure*: "Everyone I know has a big but." **Sometimes people try to hide their "buts."** They disguise them as "yeah, but" (said really fast), or think of other ways of wording "yes, but," such as "I could, but," "I would, but," and so on. If you have a "but," do not hide it. You need to show it in order to change it.

Here is a novel strategy. It is a little out there, but it will work. Smack yourself on your fabulous butt every time you say "Yes, but" or a derivative thereof (don't hurt yourself, you are just making a point). Even if you are in public, and cannot hit your own behind without attracting attention (and not the good kind!), envision doing so in your head. Envisioning the act of the butt slap or actively engaging in it might be so ridiculous that it makes you laugh, but it is also effective. Sometimes extremes are needed in order to make a change!

Yes...But Form

My BUTS!

Yes but: _____.

Yes but: _____.

Yeah but: _____.

Yeah but: _____.

I could but: _____.

I could but: _____.

I would but: _____.

I would but: _____.

Other "Buts" I'm Being Sneaky About:

_____

_____

_____

_____

Worrying and Control

Ruminating (thinking over and over and over again about a negative thought) tends to be a "stuck" behavior. You can get stuck in the cycle of worrying. Basically, the more you worry, the more you are going to worry, and the more you will be in a funk. It is not as if by some magic, worrying will cause you to be happier. That is like saying being in a funk will cause you to be fabulous. Of course it will not. You continue worrying because, in some ways, ruminating is rewarding for you.

Rewarding? That does *not* sound like it makes sense ... but it's true.

The fact is, you wouldn't worry if you didn't gain something from it. You put food in your mouth because you are rewarded for it. The food tastes good, takes your mind off your worries, gives you energy, or makes your stomach stop growling. Eating may even entertain you if you're bored. You continue eating because you are rewarded for eating. Anything rewarded increases. If a child does something inappropriate, like makes a blowing sound on his hand similar to passing gas, and you laugh at it, that kid will keep making the sound. You rewarded him with your laughter. Likewise, if your worrying is rewarded, it will increase and continue as well. Voila! There you are—rewarding yourself for being stuck in a funk.

Thus, if you want to reduce your worrying, it is important to know how your worries reward you. Ask yourself when it is that you usually worry. I bet that it is typically when you don't feel as much control over a situation as you would like, or when there are unknown factors involved. Clearly, you would be more prone to worry about a test that you've already taken, and that doesn't allow for a re-take, than one that you can take again. Knowing that you can re-take a test gives you a sense of control. Similarly, you might worry about former employees who know information about your business. They're out in the world, carrying that knowledge around with them, and you feel that you don't completely control that situation. Or, if you're in a dysfunctional or abusive relationship with someone whose behavior is unpredictable, your perception of control is less, and there are more worries. The more limited your perception of control, the more worrying takes hold.

So, most people find worrying rewarding, because it gives them a sense of control. If I were to say to you that I am going to wave a magic wand and take away all of your ability to worry, if you really think about it, your response would be panic. Suddenly, the control that you feel you have over your life would be gone. In this case, losing your worries means losing your perception of control.

But since I don't have a magic wand, you must start thinking about how the need for control affects your worrying. It is important to remember that we all have a tendency to worry more whenever stressful things are happening in our lives, because these are things that we feel are out of our control. And what happens is that everyone thinks that if they go over and over a thought, and flip it upside down, backwards, and sideways in their brain, then in some way, magically, things will be figured out. In reality we all know that a problem will not be resolved with this mental gymnastics.

However, people feel compelled to obsess and ruminate about a stressor because that act of obsessing is something that they *can* control. Though obsessing in and of itself is unpleasant, the alternative fear of feeling out of control is even worse.

If you want to reduce worries and ruminations, then you must embrace this ultimate truth: Problems will not be solved by obsessing about them. Obsessing, or ruminating, about problems will only result in a greater funk. Revisiting worries repeatedly does not give you more control, though you may feel that it does. Conversely, letting go of worrying will probably feel like a risk. But you must decrease the worrying in order to decrease the funk and be able to move on. You will need the brain space for the tools you are going to be using!

Going through life like it is a game of Pick Up Sticks is way too stressful. You cannot always be afraid of losing control and jiggling a stick. In reality, you do not have control over very many situations, anyway. It is important to figure out what you do control—and what you don't. Fix what you can when you can, but do not obsess about it. Just take action. Then, even though it feels like a risk, let go of the part that you cannot control.

Though you may feel that you are risking failure by letting go of your perceived control, really, you are not. Still, you must trust yourself. You have to be okay with a little failure if you are going to give yourself permission to take a risk. And in this case I am talking about you feeling that you are risking failure by not worrying. You may think you can control an outcome by worrying and obsessing over it. Much like feeling that wearing your lucky socks helps control whether or not your favorite football team wins or loses, those obsessions about things that you don't actually control are, in reality, a waste of time. Lucky socks or repetitive worrying are not going to control the outcome of the game. Ultimately, letting go of that responsibility is freeing.

I had a patient whose cousin was an addict and in the midst of a relapse. This cousin's relapse was causing my patient worries on several counts. My patient had been instrumental in getting this cousin a job in her husband's business, and was worried that the cousin would now try to steal from her husband, because she had relapsed and was no longer working there. The cousin had also been living with my patient's mother and helping out with the rent. A relapse meant that my patient's mother might lose her home, because of financial strain.

Clearly, my patient had many valid worries. But would my patient's worrying *change* anything about the situation? No. She needed to let go of what she couldn't change, and concentrate on changing the things she was able to affect.

In order to let go of this need to control, which leads to worrying, we must recognize what we cannot change, and make an action plan for what we *can* change. My patient could be a sounding board for her mother and help her mother think of possible solutions to her financial situation. She could suggest to her husband that he change the locks on the office. These were some solutions that resulted in my patient having *actual* control, as opposed to when she was just worrying about what her cousin *might* do.

That said, giving up that pseudo-control you get from worrying can feel risky. It may feel like you just jiggled the wrong stick in Pick Up Sticks. Give up some control, risk a little, and jiggle the wrong stick. Realize you only have so much control, anyway!

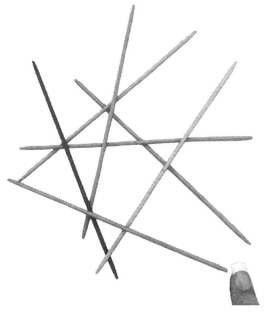

Jiggle it!

Remember, being fabulous does not mean being perfect. It means being perfectly you!

No Rewards Tool

Next, do some soul searching and circle the ways in which you are rewarded for your worrying.

- Worrying helps keep me stuck in my life.

- Worrying helps me not risk.

- Worrying helps me not have to change.

- Worrying helps me feel more in control.

- Worrying feels familiar to me, and I like familiar.

- Worrying helps me not get closer to my family.

Other:

Worrying _____.

Worrying _____.

Worrying _____.

Worrying _____.

Worrying _____.

Worrying _____.

Worrying _____.

Play Messy Tool

And . . . Play Messy!

Now, play a game of Pick Up Sticks. Choose the stick you want to pick up, then focus on the stick that you *do not* want to move. Envision the stick that you are trying to not move as representing a worry that is stuck in your head; a worry about a situation where you want control but do not have it. Then, instead of trying to not move that stick, jiggle it on purpose. This is a visual representation of loosening that thought from your brain. Then take a deep breath and realize that the world didn't end, and that you feel more relaxed now that the pressure is off. You can handle a lack of control. As a matter of fact, giving up some control and jiggling that stick can feel good!

Jiggle those sticks!
And jiggle your fabulously imperfect self!

No Control Tool Form

My current worry leading to my funk:

_____

_____

Which part of this situation can I truly control?

_____

_____

What is my action plan for this part?

_____

_____

What I do not have control over is:

_____

_____

Am I ready to let go of this? (CIrcle YES or NO)

- YES – Breathe deeply and enjoy the lighter feeling!

- NO - What do I need to do to be ready to let go of what I cannot control?

_____

_____

_____

_____

Give Yourself a "U!"

WAY TO GO!

You have completed DAY TWO!

Give yourself a

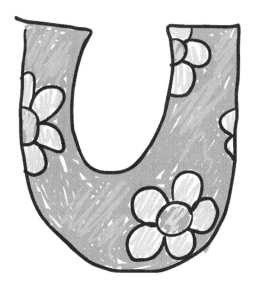

Next is beautiful:

DAY 3

Don't Should On Yourself

We have all had the experience of being caught off guard. Someone says something to us that we do not anticipate. Later, we begin thinking about what we "should have" said, "could have" said, or "would have" said. We imagine the other person's reaction when we say something so clever. We wonder what the other person would think if we'd said that. And then we chastise ourselves for being so shortsighted and unprepared. Surely, we will be better prepared next time when this exact same incident occurs. Yet, we all know that exact same incident will never occur, or that there is very little probability that it will.

The question is this: How long exactly, after an interaction has been upsetting, do you think about what you "shoulda, woulda, coulda"?

Do you have that "shoulda, woulda, coulda" thought once and then turn it off? No, of course not. If something were upsetting, such as an interaction with another person gone awry, you will replay that event many times and probably use the majority of the next day to think about it off and on.

If you have not heard the expression "don't should on yourself," you really need to make it a part of your internal repertoire. Hint: Say it aloud. Say it repeatedly to yourself! This helps to combat the funk that "shoulding" causes!

"Shoulding" leads to psychological diarrhea.

You will start with the negative thoughts and not be able to stop.

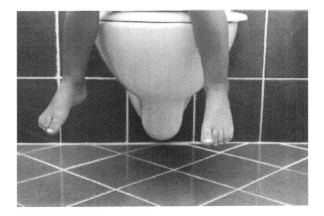

Don't Should On Yourself Tool

Instead of letting your "shoulda" worry run rampant, set a limit for yourself. Write a frequent worry that you are currently having on the "Fabulous Times Three Form." Make a tally mark when you think about it. You get three times to think of this worry, or three tally marks. The first time you worry about the subject, you must write down one positive (aka fabulous!) thought about yourself or your life. The second time you worry about the same issue, put a second tally mark, and write down two more positive and fabulous thoughts. The third and final time you worry about the same rumination, make a third tally mark, and write down three positive and fabulous things.

In order to end "Fabulous Times Three," there must be a ritual. Sing a song or do a little dance, for example. The words could be, "Oh yeah, I'm not worrying about that stupid stuff anymore, and a year from now it wouldn't matter anyway yay, yay, yay." Doing this in front of a mirror can do wonders. Also, keep your list of positive statements and refer back to them as needed for a fabulous little "pick me up." It can be as refreshing as a drink of cold water.

No "Shoulding" Tool

When you notice that you are having a "shoulda, coulda, woulda" thought, say aloud,

"I will not should on myself!"

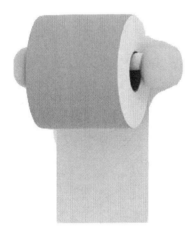

Fabulous Times Three Form

Date:_____

Frequent worry ("shoulda, coulda, woulda" thought):

_____

Tally mark one _____

One positive and fabulous thing about me or my life:

1. _____

Tally mark two_____

Two more positive and fabulous things about me or my life:

1. _____

2. _____

Tally mark three_____

Three more positive and fabulous things about me or my life:

1. _____

2. _____

3. _____

Now, I must sing a fabulous little song or dance a fabulous little dance.

My fabulous song goes like this:

_____

_____

_____

_____

I have named my fabulous dance:

_____

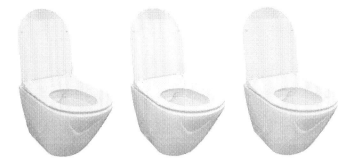

Tapping into Your Fabulous Brain

Let's talk about our fabulous brains for a minute, and the reason that negative thoughts as opposed to beautiful thoughts tend to get stuck in our minds.

We know that our brain cells, or neurons, fire when we think. It is believed that associations are made in our brain between stimuli and what we learn about those stimuli. Changes in the brain can actually happen as a result of making these associations.

In 1949, Donald Hebb came up with a theory about how cognitive, or thinking, connections are made. This theory helped explain how some thoughts become connected. Although his theory has been studied and refined, even after all of this time, it is still inspiring. We can think of it as a general framework for neural connections in the brain. Basically, when our brains learn something new, neurons, or brain cells, become activated. They then make connections with other neurons. According to Hebb's theory, we make an association in our brain between stimuli and what we learn about those stimuli. Part of his theory is often paraphrased as "Neurons that fire together wire together."

Simply stated, that means if we see something small and green, and we hear that the name for this small green thing is "frog," an association is made in our brain between the visual stimuli of this small green thing and the stimuli of the word "frog." The same associations appear to be made between stimuli, thought (or cognitive response), and emotion.

It makes sense that the more emotional an event, the less exposure that you need to have to that event to remember it. If an event is low on the emotional scale, you may not recall it as well. For example, if you first meet someone with dark, curly hair and brown eyes and hear that the name of that person is Amber, you may need to hear the name associated with that person more than once in order to form the neuronal connection, in part because you haven't made any emotional connection to her. We have all had the experience of meeting new people and immediately forgetting their name. Hearing a new name is pretty low on the emotional event scale.

In regard to a more emotional occurrence, if you ride a blue scooter for the first time and fall and break your wrist, you may have difficulty looking at a blue scooter without the memory of that painful event. An immediate and strongly emotional connection was made in that instance. That connection then becomes even more reinforced because you think of it often. Repeating the event mentally when you fell from the blue scooter and injured yourself makes the association between blue scooter and injury even stronger. Also, since the fall from the scooter is different from the routine of daily life, and is a dramatically unique incident, it stands out in your mind.

On the flip side, an emotional connection can be also be made with a positive event. If, for example, you had a heartwarming time at Disney with your family, a connection is made between Disney and feelings of family and happiness. Later, seeing a picture of Cinderella's castle can conjure up the emotionally wonderful time you had at Disney.

Clearly, positive memories and thoughts can stay with you, as opposed to only negative ones.

However, in order to reinforce positive neuronal connections, the connections in your brain that allow you to remember positive thoughts, you must replay the positive experiences and emotions many times in your mind. Obviously, this positive mental replay should happen without also searching for negative memories. Unfortunately, the temptation is to think more about the scooter accident than Cinderella's castle. We somehow believe that thinking about the negative incident will make sense of what happened. Thinking about the scooter incident more than the castle gets back to obsessing in order to try to control negative things that already happened. Obsessing about the past in order to control it is, of course, completely irrational. And, unfortunately, the more that we have a thought, the deeper the connections in our brain about that thought become. Which can lead to more ruminating about the negative thought.

The fact that the scooter accident was emotionally stimulating may also help it get stuck in our brains. But the cool thing is that not only negative, but also positive events can be emotionally stimulating. So, it is possible to tap into the positive emotional events more than the negative. It is possible to think more about the family's day at Disney than the scooter accident. You can purposely train your brain to be more fabulous than funk. A big problem is that those negative thoughts have become a stronger association in your brain from thinking so much about them. This emphasizes the importance of doing just the opposite: Thinking repeatedly about the *positive* events instead. You want the positive events to become more embedded in your brain than the negative ones. You want the fabulous to start coming more easily!

Sometimes, people find that they are simply uncomfortable when they do not have depression or are not in a funk. When a moment occurs when they do not have the depression, they look for that funk. A funk may be miserable, but it is a known entity. If it's gone, people feel like they've lost their foundation. Which leads them right back into focusing on the negative connections.

We also have a tendency to look for cognitively dissonant thoughts because our brains are basically wired to worry. Looking for what does not make sense in our world is linked to survival and our innate fight or flight instinct. However, most of us do not have to constantly run for our lives, or fight every day to survive. But our brains still push us in the negative direction of worrying.

Often, people will take the known funk over everything else because it feels safer.

You must trust yourself that you *will* be okay without your depressive funk. When you get that "brain space" from not focusing on the negative connections, be prepared to fill it with some good stuff! Having a ready arsenal of positive thoughts, feelings, and experiences in your tool belt is your best defense against returning to the funk. Assemble the "thought items" to fill your head, like fabulous thoughts, images, and words, so that they're ready and raring to go!

Tapping Into Your Fabulous Brain Tool

Write down five events in the last month that led to positive emotions for you. These do not have to be big things. Positive emotion examples include thrilled, happy, content, excited, surprised, cheerful, elated, and more—even fabulous! Your events could include, "I felt content when my husband hugged me," or "I felt bright when I saw the ray of sun." If you have difficulty thinking of five things in the last month that led to positive emotions for you, then go back six months or a year. Now you know that your daily focus is to look for and remember the positive emotions you have. Your goal is to work up to writing down one to five instances of emotionally positive events a day. It is very important to not just list the event, but to also include the positive emotion associated with that event. The "Positive Emotion Logs" will help keep you on track. And the "Positive Feeling Word Bank" will provide you with scrumptiously positive words at the ready!

Don't crumple up and throw away your
positive emotions; hang onto them!

Positive Emotion Logs

POSITIVE EMOTION LOG: DAILY

Today's Date:_____

I felt _____ when _____.

I felt _____ when _____.

I felt _____ when _____.

I felt _____ when _____.

I felt _____ when _____.

I felt _____ when _____.

I felt _____ when _____.

I felt _____ when _____.

I felt _____ when _____.

I felt _____ when _____.

I felt _____ when _____.

I felt _____ when _____.

I felt _____ when _____.

I felt _____ when _____.

I felt _____ when _____.

I felt _____ when _____.

I felt _____ when _____.

I felt _____ when _____.

I felt _____ when _____.

I felt _____ when _____.

POSITIVE EMOTION LOG: WEEKLY

Week's Date:_____

Sunday:

I felt _____ when _____.

I felt _____ when _____.

I felt _____ when _____.

I felt _____ when _____.

I felt _____ when _____.

Monday:

I felt _____ when _____.

I felt _____ when _____.

I felt _____ when _____.

I felt _____ when _____.

I felt _____ when _____.

Tuesday:

I felt _____ when _____.

I felt _____ when _____.

I felt _____ when _____.

I felt _____ when _____.

I felt _____ when _____.

Wednesday:

I felt _____ when _____.

I felt _____ when _____.

I felt _____ when _____.

I felt _____ when _____.

I felt _____ when _____.

Thursday:

I felt _____ when _____.

I felt _____ when _____.

I felt _____ when _____.

I felt _____ when _____.

I felt _____ when _____.

Friday:

I felt _____ when _____..

I felt _____ when _____.

I felt _____ when _____.

I felt _____ when _____.

I felt _____ when _____.

Saturday:

I felt _____ when _____.

I felt _____ when _____.

I felt _____ when _____.

I felt _____ when _____.

I felt _____ when _____.

Positive Feeling Word Bank

Fabulous, thrilled, happy, content, excited, surprised, cheerful, elated, bubbly, giddy, calm, comfortable, safe, relaxed, confident, responsible, peaceful, caring, delighted, jolly, tickled, silly, proud, joyful, thankful, great, loved, loving, blissful, grateful.

Use your own words, and feel free to make some up that feel good to you!

Like ... fantabulous!

_____, _____, _____,

_____, _____, _____,

_____, _____, _____,

and keep going!!!

Sparks

Sparks are positive, fleeting thoughts. They may take you off guard, but do not ignore them. Write them down immediately or you might forget! You may not expect to have these thoughts, and the thoughts may be so foreign to you that you discredit them when they occur. A Spark may be, "Wow, I have my entire life in front of me to do with as I like!" or even "I have the entire day to do with as I like!" A Spark may be a really cool, profound thought with which you surprise yourself. Or, it might be an awesome realization about yourself.

If you start analyzing your Sparks, you may find that they tend to occur in a certain place, or at a certain time. I have noticed that I often have Spark-ly moments when I am in the water. Water is a fabulous place for me. I tend to be relaxed and pretty happy in these moments, and the Sparks start flying!

Respect the Sparks. Remember them. The more you focus on your Sparks, the less fleeting they will be, and the more Spark-ly and fabulous you will become!

Spark-ly Thoughts Tool

Keep track of all of your Sparks! Then analyze them. At what time did the Spark happen? Were you tired or rested? Remember, it is possible to have a Spark-ly thought even when you are in a funk. Pay attention to any and all Sparks!

To analyze your sparks, you will need to note some things, and to do that you can use your "Sparkle Log." First, simply list the Spark-ly thought. Next, note the day, date, and time. Finally, list what was going on when you had your Spark. This could include the location (sitting in the grass), your physical state (relaxed, too tired to worry), or your emotion at the time (had been laughing at a joke, felt contented, etc.).

After you have gathered about seven of your Sparks, let the analysis begin! How often do they occur? The more you pay attention to them, and document them, the more often they will occur. Spark-ly thoughts love attention!

Help make your Sparks happen. Go hang out under an inspiring tree or wherever they tend to happen. Don't forget your favorite pen and "Sparkle Log," so you can document those Sparks!

When you are having a downer moment, refer back to your Sparks. Read them, believe them, and internalize them. Do not just notice and document your Sparks, but actually use them! Believing in your Sparks equals believing in yourself!

SPARKLE LOG

I had a Spark-ly thought! Here it is:

_____.

Date: _____Day: _____

Time: _____

When I had my Spark, I was

_____.

(Note location, your physical state, or emotion)

I had a Spark-ly thought! Here it is:

_____.

Date: _____Day: _____

Time:_____

When I had my Spark, I was

_____.

(Note location, your physical state, or emotion)

I had a Spark-ly thought! Here it is:

_____.

Date: _____Day: _____

Time:_____

When I had my Spark, I was

_____.

(Note location, your physical state, or emotion)

I had a Spark-ly thought! Here it is:

_____.

Date: _____Day: _____

Time:_____

When I had my Spark, I was

_____.

(Note location, your physical state, or emotion)

Give Yourself an "N!"

YOU ROCK!

You have completed DAY THREE!

Give yourself an

I know you can't wait for sparkly:

DAY 4

Replaying Negative Events

I have seen people in therapy who, given the horribly traumatizing events they have experienced in their lives, amaze me with their ability to function on a daily basis. They truly inspire me. I will not relate to you examples of these traumatizing events, because I do not want them in your head. Obviously, though, these events are difficult for people to stop replaying in their minds. The problem is, the more they do replay those memories, the more embedded the memories become. Soldiers coming back from combat also often have difficulty going about day-to-day business. Even if they have not developed post-traumatic stress disorder, depression can still be evident. One cause of the depression may stem from the soldiers' tendency to replay the memories of what they've experienced.

It appears that the less control you have over something that happens to you, and the more stressful or traumatizing it is to you emotionally, the more that memory will be replayed in your mind. If you have undergone a stressful event in your life, such as a traumatic death in your family, you may very well have difficulty working through it without therapy. You probably felt a desperate lack of control over what happened. And you likely *still* feel like you need to try to figure out how you could have had more control.

When my father died, it was sudden; he was fine, then he was in the hospital, and then hospice for a week. How he "suddenly" had metastatic cancer all over his body was never explained, and I was not in charge of the medical decisions. I felt like I'd been left in the dark. My father was dying and I had hardly any opportunity to speak with him. I felt utterly out of control, and could easily be haunted by what I "shoulda, woulda, coulda" done to somehow save his life. I know, though, that to think that I could have saved his life in that situation is an irrational thought.

To let something that felt out of control remain unresolved in your mind is quite the trick. But replaying that negative memory is not going to resolve the problem. What ruminating about that negative memory *will* do is make you more miserable and depressed. It will contribute to the overall funk with which you go about your day-to-day life.

Worrying Is Like Brain Erosion

I lived on a small parcel of acreage in Texas as an adult for about twelve years. Growing up in Florida, I did not really understand the concept of erosion, given that Florida is basically made of sand. However, in our area of Texas, clay was predominant. Erosion would occur whenever the clay was exposed and dry. Every time it rained, the rain tended to find its way down a certain path through the dirt. These rivulets would become deeper and deeper every time it rained. In much the same way, neuronal (brain cell) paths may become more and more worn in our brains. When we obsess, or ruminate, on thoughts, the links between one thought to another become stronger. In essence, it's just like erosion. The thoughts become deeper and deeper in our brains, more definitively linked, and thus harder to resist. It is so much easier to go from one negative thought to another. You are digging a pathway that helps you live in the depressive funk.

The next time you begin to mull over, then obsess about, a depressing or sad situation, I want you to imagine that your ruminations are eroding your brain! Remember, worry leads to more worry. Happiness leads to more happiness!

This is your brain on worrying!

Start Planning!

Right now I want you to think of a worry that you often have. Do not actually worry about it—just think of the topic. Without even going through the process of worrying about that situation, you can probably tell me what you start off thinking about initially, and what each subsequent worrisome thought is.

For example, a person in a dysfunctional relationship might think of worries like so: First: "I need to leave my partner." Second: "I don't have any money." Third: "I should've listened to my parents and gotten a better education." Fourth: "I don't have any money to get an education, now." Fifth: "The move will be hard on my children." Six: "Staying in this relationship is hard on my children." Seven: "How might I support my children?" Eight: "I have no money, why didn't I listen to my parents and get a better education?" Thus, the cycle of guilt and worry repeats itself and continues.

There is a difference between problem solving and worrying.

You might ask, if this person has so many problems but does not have these negative thoughts, how will the person ever find a way out of this problematic situation? The answer is that the person must stop with the worrying and start with the problem solving.

Problem solving is *constructive*, and worrying is *destructive*.

Taking a problem and making a plan helps turn the funk of worrying into the plan of fabulous! If you take a certain amount of time every day in order to problem solve and make a plan, instead of beating yourself down and becoming exhausted with worry, you can become more constructive! The person in the above example may even be able to eventually start a new life.

Start Planning Tool!

You must find the most daunting task or situation hanging over you and make a plan to conquer it. This could include where to go next in your career, education, or love life. Worrying about these situations will only produce funk and inhibit fabulousness, and if you try to ignore them, your biggest worries will find a way to seep into your brain and weigh you down during the day.

Instead of worrying, problem-solve. Be constructive. Make a plan! Use the "Master Plan Plan," "Brainstorming Sheet," and "Timeline" for guidance.

Step One: Identify the Problem. For example, you may be dissatisfied with your career as a veterinary nurse.

Step Two: Brainstorm! Write all over the Brainstorming page with possibilities that come to mind. Do not criticize any of your ideas. Just generate them! Brainstorming ideas can include finishing veterinary school, going into the computer field, or becoming a therapeutic yoga instructor.

Step Three: Sift! Go through each Brainstorm idea and see which one or ones you like the best. You may be passionate about yoga, feel that it has made a positive impact on your health and your life, and believe that you have a knack for it. As a veterinary nurse, you have a working knowledge of biology that could help you be effective as a therapeutic yoga instructor for people with health problems or are differently abled.

Step Four: Answer the questions "What?" "When?" "Where?" and "How?" for each brainstorming idea you have picked. Check out the example below!

<u>What is it that I am going to do first?</u>

Research and choose a training program.

<u>When am I going to do it?</u>

In one year, when I will have saved enough money for the training program by putting away a certain amount of money each month.

<u>Where is this part of the plan going to take place?</u>

(Identify the location of the training program.)

<u>How will I make this part of the plan happen?</u>

I will time this so that my apartment's rental contract ends at the same time that the program starts, since I will have to be at a different location for the school. I will then make my resume and find a job at a yoga studio as an instructor in a town where I have wanted to live, but to which I have not had the courage to move.

Write your Ultimate Goal above!

You can be broad with your ideas at first, and then become more detailed with your plans later on. Your plan may not be quite as grandiose as the example provided, but don't be afraid to think big! Also, sometimes plans, or parts of plans, change, so be flexible. Revisit your "Master Plan Plan" as time goes on to determine whether you still like the idea, or want to tweak it.

Master Plan Plan

Step One: Identify the Problem.

Step Two: Brainstorm! (See Brainstorming sheet)

Step Three: Sift! Go through each Brainstorm idea and see which one or ones you like the best.

Step Four: Answer the questions "What?" "When?" "Where?" and "How?" for each brainstorming idea you have picked.

What is it that I'm going to do first?

When am I going to do it? (See Timeline)

Where is this part of the plan going to take place?

How will I make this part of the plan happen?

Brainstorming Sheet

Dear Person,

Please write all over me. Do not leave any part of me blank. Write big, write small, write fancy, write messy. I want it all!

Love,

Your Brainstorming Sheet

P.S. Thanks! Great job!

Timeline

Use this timeline to help answer the **WHEN** question of Step Four of your Master Plan Plan.

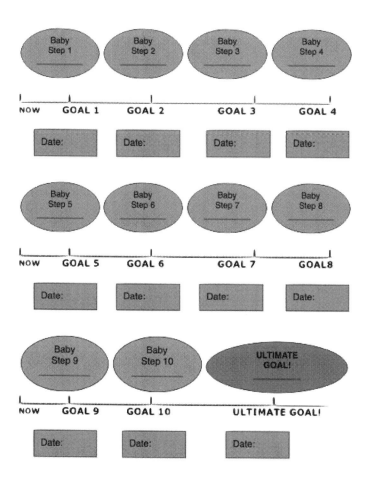

Focusing on the Negative Funk

Here's another brain buster. We tend to focus on thoughts that are more cognitively dissonant, or unresolved, in our minds. When things do not make sense to us, they do not fit into the schema that we have developed in our minds about how life is and how life should go. We have a natural inclination to focus on those cognitively dissonant events more. Trying to pull the thoughts together in our brains that do not make sense causes more of a funk. Allowing negative things to *not make sense* in our brains frees us up more to be fabulous.

People that are depressed usually expect things to go extremely well during their day. Thus, when things do not go perfectly, they tend to become very angry. I have a patient who came into the office extremely agitated about how some people in a car had behaved as the patient was on his way to his appointment with me. He discussed how furious he was at these people, and how the individuals should not have behaved as they did. He could only talk about their ignorance and rudeness. The more he tried to resolve the lack of congruity between his expectations for people's behavior, and the reality, the more upset he became. I have another patient who becomes extremely angry at the weather. If it rains when he needs to walk from one place to another, he will rant about the unfairness of life. He also becomes upset about construction if he is not able to get from one place to another within the timeframe that he expects. Both of these patients worry and are then angry all day about the car, the weather, and the construction. Have you heard the expression, "That just ruined my day!"?

In the above examples, my patients chose to focus on one negative aspect of their entire day, because it did not fit with their expectations. The fact that my patient had an amazing therapy session immediately following the traffic issue was not his focus. He does not spend all day thinking about the fact that he had a great conversation with his girlfriend, or that he has shelter and food. People seem to feel there is more validity to focusing on the bad stuff that happens during the day than thinking about their good stuff. Some feel superior because they spend more time thinking about conflicting thoughts. It is as if they believe that thinking about the good stuff is not worthy of brain space or would somehow make them simple-minded. What? A funk is more thought-worthy than fabulousness? Wrong. We all need to be thoughtful and thankful for any good stuff that happens during the day, big or small.

One of my favorite mottos is: **"Be prepared for everything but don't expect anything."**

Be prepared for the rain by bringing an umbrella, or changing your opinion about being wet, but don't expect for it to rain or not rain. Being controlling about life and having narrow expectations generally leads to unhappiness. You will never be able to control external forces—only your internal response to them. Your "luck" does not have to change in order for you to be happy.

Do not expect to change the world to make yourself more comfortable; change your response to the world, and your world will change.

Fab Good Stuff

Something extravagantly fabulous does not happen in your life on a moment-to-moment or day-to-day basis. You do not go to Disney every day. You do not even go to the movies or out to eat every day. However, every day there is at least *one* tiny little fab thing. Like you saw a pretty butterfly. Or your loved one smiled. Having shelter, food, and clothing aren't half bad, either.

At one point, I worked with a little girl who had mood problems, and of course, resulting behavior problems. I asked her to tell me her Good Stuff every time I saw her. She always had significant difficulty answering this question. One day, when I asked her what her Good Stuff was, she told me that she had seen a beautiful ladybug on a leaf. I knew then that we were making progress. And I haven't looked at a ladybug the same way since.

If you wait for something fabulous to happen to you, then you will never be fabulous. You must notice the fabulousness that is already around you. By doing this, you will start developing the ability to notice the fabulousness within you. It will begin bubbling up from the inside!

Good Stuff Bad Stuff Tool

Every day, I want you to notice "good stuff" and "bad stuff" that happens in your life. Put these things in your Fab Good Stuff and Funk Bad Stuff folders in your brain. Create them now. What color is your Fab Good Stuff folder? Place it where it goes in your brain. What color is your Funk Bad Stuff folder? Place that folder where it goes in your brain. Now, every day, put the good stuff—your "Lil Fabs"—in the Fab Good Stuff folder, and the bad stuff that happens in the Funk Bad Stuff folder. Then, I want you to set the Funk Bad Stuff folder on a shelf in your brain. I want you to return to your Fab Good Stuff folder at least three times during the day to look at all of your Lil Fabs. You can use your "Good Stuff Bad Stuff Forms." Lil Fabs are fun to collect! Start now!

Good Stuff Bad Stuff Forms

FABULOUS GOOD STUFF—"Lil Fabs"

Week's Date:_____

Sunday:
Keep giving these a peek!

_____, _____, _____

Monday:
Keep giving these a peek!

_____, _____, _____

Tuesday:

Keep giving these a peek!

_____, _____, _____

Wednesday:

Keep giving these a peek!

_____, _____, _____

Thursday:

Keep giving these a peek!

_____, _____, _____

Friday:

Keep giving these a peek!

_____, _____, _____

Saturday:

Keep giving these a peek!

_____, _____, _____

FUNK BAD STUFF

Week's Date:_____

Sunday:

_____, _____, _____ SHELVE IT!

Monday:

_____, _____, _____ SHELVE IT!

Tuesday:

_____, _____, _____ SHELVE IT!

Wednesday:

_____, _____, _____ SHELVE IT!

Thursday:

_____, _____, _____ SHELVE IT!

Friday:

_____, _____, _____ SHELVE IT!

Saturday:

_____, _____, _____ **SHELVE IT!**

Zoning Out and Opening Doors

Right now, you probably catch yourself worrying after you have already been worrying for ten minutes or more. You are completely unproductive during this time, likely staring off into space or at your computer screen. You are feeding the funk when this happens, and starving your fabulousness.

Visualize this:

When you start worrying, it is like you are walking down a weedy path. You eventually get to a semi-semicircular room, which is in your brain. In this semi-circular room you see many doors. Each door, once opened, leads to the other. Let's use the earlier example of the person who wants to end a dysfunctional relationship. That person's brain would have eight doors. This person would walk down that "weedy path" to the brain's worry room, and open the first door, behind which are worries about needing to leave the partner. These worries lead to opening the second door. In the second room are money worries. This leads to the third door being opened, and out of that pour worries about not having a better education, which may have helped this person find a job more easily. Then, the fourth door opens and the person enters it thinking about not having the financial resources to get an education now. Behind the fifth door the person uncovers worries about not giving the children a better life, and how the move would be hard on them. And so on. . . .

Here is another example. The first door might open and you find yourself thinking about owing more on your house than what it is worth. This would lead to the second door opening, which would make you think that you made a terrible decision to buy the house at the peak of the real estate market. Then the third door opens, and you think foreclosing on this house would be shameful. The next door includes foreclosing on the house and how that would also ruin your credit. The final door may entail you thinking about what a *loser* you are because you have "ruined" your children's life through this situation. Clearly, opening one worry door can quickly lead to opening *multiple* worry doors. And with that, we start to see escalations of worrying. And negative self-talk is sure to follow, such as thinking about oneself in terms of being a "loser."

Obviously, the person trying to manage an unintended problem is not a loser. Having the courage to confront a difficult situation is many times nothing short of heroic. Unfortunately, though, self-punishing thoughts crop up during bouts of worry.

Closing the Doors Tool

When you realize that you're worrying, even if you have been worrying for ten minutes, visualize yourself shutting the doors in your brain and backing down the weedy path that you have walked. Then distract yourself. It is okay to distract yourself from your worrying if you have set aside a time to actually worry during the day.

It may be shocking that I am telling you to worry during the day. However, it is important for you to have a specified "Worry Time" every day. Most people's problem is not that they worry, but that they worry in a messy way. Your biggest problem is probably that you need to clean up your worrying. But first, it is important to practice shutting the doors in your brain, or not opening them in the first place. Use "My Distraction List" to help distract you from the worries, which helps to shut those doors. Continue on to "How to Worry" to learn more about, well, how to worry!

MY DISTRACTION LIST

Refer to this list when you need to distract yourself!

Ways I might distract myself:

Read a book, play cards, sing a song, go for a walk, play a video game, watch TV, etc.

These activities help me close the doors to my worries:

_____

_____

_____

Distract Yourself After You Close Your Doors to Your Worries!

How To Worry

I'm not going to tell you how not to worry. I want you to know how to worry. Most people have no idea how to worry properly. They keep trying to not worry at all, and end up worrying more. Furthermore, telling someone not to worry about something is completely unrealistic. If those kinds of superpowers were possible, spandex companies would be working in overdrive (you know, for all of the superhero outfits)!

While knowing how to whittle down your worrying is super important (coming up soon in "Being Happy Is Like Resisting Chocolate. . . Huh?"), it is just as important to know what to do with those daily worry leftovers. So for now, let's talk about the business of how to worry. Currently, your worrying is probably messy and needs to be cleaned up. Organizing your worrying will reduce your funk time and make more room for fabulousness in your brain!

Choose a Time

First, you need to pick a time, every day, when you are going to focus on your worries. I suggest you choose a time of day that fits with your schedule almost every day of the week. It is important that, for at least the first two weeks, you keep the exact same timing every day.

Pick a Place

Second, pick a place where you are going to worry. Your "worry place" should be in a spot where you only go to worry at your appointed Worry Time. Some people never sit at their dining room table. This is a spot that could be a worry area. Another possible area is on your back porch, or in your back yard or under a tree. Some like to worry when they are in the shower, and they imagine their worries running down the drain. Others like to worry when they are driving to class or work. Yet another option is to go for walks and worry.

Do not choose your worry place as your bed. You will train your brain to worry in the bed and then may have problems falling asleep at night.

Hot Seat

Sometimes a special chair or stool, which we refer to as the "hot seat," is beneficial to have in your worry place. That way, when you are on your "hot seat" you will be more likely to worry, and out of your "hot seat" you will be less likely to worry. You may even eventually forget about worrying all together when you are not on your "hot seat!"

By assigning your Worry Time to a certain place and time, you are training your brain. It is best if we pair the same time with the same place to worry every day. Thus, when you are in your "hot seat" on the back porch at 5:30 every afternoon, your brain knows that it is time to worry. By the same token, when you are *not* in your worry place at your worry time of day, your brain is not as likely to be triggered to worry.

Limit Your Worry Time

You get a half-hour to worry, max. That's it. It is of utmost importance to limit your Worry Time. Before you sit down on your "hot seat" to worry, set a timer for thirty minutes. Depending on the intensity of the particular worries, some people can tolerate five minutes, or fifteen minutes, instead of thirty, which is fine. Sometimes, if the is shorter, such as five minutes, I will have the person worry two to three times during the day, such as in the morning and then in the afternoon. The Worry Time cannot be too close to bedtime. We do not want to intrude upon your fabulous sleep! You need it!

During your Worry Time, pull out your Worry Log (described in the next section), read over everything that you have written about your worries during the day, and worry about every single thing. You can cry, you can yell, or anything else you'd like while reading your worries. Some people like to make a plan to problem solve during this time. Some people pray. If you are using this time to problem solve, then you need to write down your solutions. Once they are written down, you are not allowed to ruminate about the solution or the problem—unless it's your Worry Time, of course!

Distracting Activity

Before you sit down for your Worry Time, plan on a distracting activity for the end of your Worry Time. Otherwise, your worrying may bleed over outside of your Worry Time. A distracting activity may include making dinner, watching your favorite show, or playing a card game. When the timer goes off at the end of your five, fifteen, or thirty-minute Worry Time, proceed to your distracting activity.

Refer to "My Distraction List." And keep on adding to it with fabulously distracting activities!

Jot and Go!

Carry with you a worry log, like the one provided here. Every time that you have a worry, write down your worry, and then put the log away. You may also write your worries on a tiny book you stick in your back pocket, or the notes section of your cell phone. If you do use your phone or another electronic device, please make sure that it is password protected, because these worries are no one else's business.

When you write down each worry, you don't need to write a book. Jot down a short phrase instead. You will know what that worry is after reading just a few words about it, because you probably have that worry all the time. There is no need to elaborate. The elaboration that you give that particular worry will take place during your appointed Worry Time, as described above.

Again, you may be worrying for ten minutes by the time you realize that you are worrying. Still, follow the same rules, and write down your worry as soon as you realize that you are worrying. After you have written down your worry, distract yourself. Jot and go on with your day! I have a patient with a severe and paralyzing fear of bugs. Even seeing one tiny bug can send her into a tailspin. Now that she is better about stopping the obsessive worrying after spying a bug, she has learned that the next step is to move on, which can be difficult to accept. Moving on from a worry is hard. Jotting that worry down, so that you don't feel that you have to keep it in your brain, and then using a distracting activity can help.

Distracting activities could include singing to yourself, playing a video game, reading, walking outside, or any other activity you find distracting. What works for one person may not work for another, so create your own list of fabulous distractions! Record them in your Distraction List, for future use.

I have often heard the suggestion of envisioning a large red stop sign when it is time to stop a particular thought. However, I find that trying to see a stop sign in one's mind is not as beneficial as distraction activities, because trying to imagine a stop sign is another cognitive task. Worrying, of course, is a largely cognitive, or thinking, activity. Adding a thinking activity in order to distract yourself from another thinking activity generated by your own brain does not usually work well. When physical motion is involved, especially along with something you find interesting, you'll find a distraction to be more successful. If you cannot be physically active, a more passive cognitive activity requiring outside stimuli, such as watching a show, playing a computer game, or computer work, helps with distraction. Remember, even singing your own fabulous song and dancing your own fabulous little dance involves movement and thought! And, even better, they come from fabulous you!

Your Worry Method

So, in a nutshell, here is your worry method. Every time you catch yourself worrying, write the worry down in your "Worry Log." Then, put it away. Distract yourself. Take your worry log out when it is your Worry Time, and review all the worries. Remember, make sure you have Worry Time in the same location every day, and at the same time of day. The place you pick should only be used for the Worry Time. Allow yourself thirty minutes max. You may choose to worry for five, fifteen, or thirty minutes, but set your timer for your Worry Time length. When the timer goes off, you must distract yourself and stop worrying! Plan your Worry Time distraction activity ahead of time, so it's ready to go the second your Worry Time is up.

Don't forget that establishing a new habit or behavior takes work. This technique must be used every day. You will not make new pathways in your brain, or establish new thinking habits, without daily dedicated work. Who becomes fabulous without some work? No one!

Worry Routine Guide

Use this sheet as a guide for establishing your WORRY ROUTINE. Your routine may remain the same after you set it the first week, or you may want to make some adjustments to it. If your life schedule changes, then don't just drop your WORRY TIME! Change your WORRY ROUTINE!

Week ONE
Date:_____

My worry time is:

_____ (Example, 5:00pm)

My worry place is:

_____ (Example, stool on the back porch)

I will worry for:

_____ minutes (Example, 5, 15, or 30 minutes)

My pre-planned distraction activity after my worry time is:

_____

Week TWO

Date:_____

My worry time is: _____

My worry place is: _____

I will worry for: _____ minutes

My pre-planned distraction activity after my worry time is:

_____

Week THREE

Date:_____

My worry time is: _____

My worry place is: _____

I will worry for: _____ minutes

My pre-planned distraction activity after my worry time is:

_____

Worry Log

List worries you are having throughout the day

Worries I am having TODAY
Date: _____

Worry #1:

_____

Distraction used:

_____

Worry #2:

_____

Distraction used:

_____

Worry #3:

_____

Distraction used:

_____

Worry #4:

_____

Distraction used:

_____

Worry #5:

_____

Distraction used:

_____

Worry #6:

_____

Distraction used:

_____

Review the above worries and worry about them during your appointed worry time.

Give Yourself a "K!"

AWESOME!

You have completed DAY FOUR!

Give yourself a

Brace yourself for bodacious:

DAY 5

Being Happy Is Like Resisting Chocolate. . . Huh?

What we don't often realize is that worrying is *tempting*. Just like we may know that we should not have a piece of chocolate cake when we are on a diet (or are allergic to chocolate, or are avoiding gluten, or other reasons to avoid the glorious chocolate cake) we want it. And we want it now. It's extremely difficult to resist something so tempting when it is sitting right in front of us. Worrying is much the same. We know that avoiding the excessive worrying is what we *should* do, much as we should avoid the chocolate cake. But it is difficult to *not* worry when that worry is sitting right in front of us.

Although worries are definitely not as pleasant as chocolate cake, they are just as tempting. When you are trying to change your thinking to more positive thought patterns, it is necessary to actively resist worrying when it is not your Worry Time. Withstanding the urge to worry is like resisting a big decadent piece of chocolate cake that you know is not good for you.

Let's say that a negative thought is there in your brain. You know that worry is sitting in front of you, just waiting to be chewed over and over again. And an opportunity to torture yourself with a piece of worry cake can sometimes be difficult to ignore. Who can turn down that kind of temptation? Worry cake is so deliciously full of ooey gooey guilt and unresolved angst. It just keeps you coming back for more. Staying on your worry diet can feel difficult. Why?!

One fact about worries that makes them difficult to resist is that worrying is immediate. If you have a worry in your mind, you have the ability to think about it right away. Changing your way of thinking is not as immediately reinforcing (or rewarding) as worrying is. When we really want that piece of cake, it is so very rewarding because it tastes great instantaneously. And when we want to worry about something, the worrying is rewarding because we get to obsess about the problem right away. We do not have to wait.

However, we must wait to worry at a specified time during our Worry Time in order to change our worrying.

As we know, any behavior that is rewarded, or reinforced, increases. And the quicker the reward, the better. Rewarding, or reinforcing, our puppy right away with a treat for standing on her hind legs is going to get her to repeat that behavior far more quickly than rewarding the puppy an hour after she has danced on her hind legs.

Similarly, resisting that nagging, negative pull of the worry cake is like denying yourself a tempting and immediate reward that is sitting right in front of you. And, unlike eating the cake, resisting the temptation doesn't bring you immediate gratification. For example, when people try to diet, it is difficult, because putting that food into their mouths is so immediately rewarding. You don't have to wait for the food to taste good when you eat it. The food tastes good right away. Seeing weight loss down the road takes a long time. It is not an immediate reward.

Worrying right away is like taking a bite of that chocolate cake. It fulfills a need, or a hunger, that you think you have. That hunger is usually an urge to gain control, or to punish yourself. It is tempting to do, but if you take that bite, weight loss (or rather, worry loss) gets further away.

The same goes for changing worry patterns. Worrying when the thought hits you is difficult to resist. If you give in and worry, then happiness and fabulousness are further away.

It will take longer to change those worry patterns. However, if you have the willpower to *not* worry right away, write down your worry, and think about it at your designated Worry Time, then that change to the fabulousness you crave will happen!

Being Happy Is Like Resisting Chocolate... Huh? Tool

The key is to reward yourself for resisting a negative thought, and *not* reward yourself for giving in. What is something that you really want to work toward? You will get "resist points" every time you resist a worry.

First, decide on a "small reward" for yourself. The only criterion is that it must be something you really want. Is it a banana split, to watch a sports game on TV, order out a pizza, read some of your new book, or take a bubble bath? Your small reward is something you can have daily at the end of the day, if you are successful for that day.

Next, pick a "BIG reward." A BIG reward would be a pair of shoes, for example. Giving yourself free time on the weekend to do something that you love like art, going to the beach, or fishing may also be a BIG reward for you. Set the amount of successful days that you need in order to receive your BIG reward. You might require that you have five out of seven successful reward days, for example, to get your BIG reward. Do not make yourself wait too long for your BIG reward, especially at first! And do not make it all or nothing. If, out of seven days, you had five successful days, you deserve a reward!

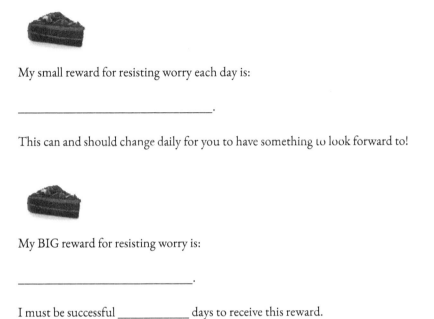

My small reward for resisting worry each day is:

_____.

This can and should change daily for you to have something to look forward to!

My BIG reward for resisting worry is:

_____.

I must be successful _____ days to receive this reward.

My Big and Small Rewards

About the small rewards:

Your "small" reward is something you can have at the end of the day, if you are successful for that day. A "small" reward could be a bubble bath, watching a TV show, or reading a book, for example. Your small rewards will keep you going!

Possible "small" rewards for resisting worrying (to be rewarded at the end of each day of *MY RESISTANCE!*) are:

_____, _____, _____

_____, _____, _____

My small reward for resisting worry each day this week is:

_____.

This can and should change daily or weekly for you to have something to look forward to!

About the BIG rewards:

Pick a "BIG reward." A "BIG reward" would be a pair of shoes, or several hours on the weekend to do something you like (painting, fishing, etc.). Set how many successful days you need for this BIG reward. You might require yourself to have five out of seven successful reward days to get your BIG reward, for example. Remember, do not make yourself wait too long for your BIG reward, especially at first!

Possible "BIG" rewards for resisting worrying (to be rewarded at the end of the first week of *MY RESISTANCE!*) are:

_____, _____, _____

_____, _____, _____

Now narrow it down and pick one for your first seven-day resistance reward!

My BIG reward for resisting worry is: _____.

I must be successful _____days to receive this reward (Example, five out of seven days).

Measuring the Success of Your Resistance

How do you measure success? In order to have a successful day, you must have a certain number of RESIST POINTS. You earn a RESIST POINT each time you feel the need to worry but refuse to do so.

Make a tally mark here for each time you resist a worry: _____.

Now add up your marks at the end of the day, right before you would receive your reward.

I resisted _____ time(s) today.

Did you resist enough times to get your reward?

Remember, start off slowly, and do not place goals too high at first. Give yourself a break. For the first day, if you resisted one time, you were successful. Yay!

Refer to "My Resistance Forms!" to help you keep track!

So. . .

Week One and Two: You are successful EACH DAY if you successfully resist a worry one time. You receive your daily small reward!

Week One and Two: If you have been successful FIVE out of SEVEN DAYS in resisting a worry, you get your BIG reward!

Week Three and Four: You are successful EACH DAY if you successfully resist a worry two times. You receive your daily small reward!

Week Three and Four: If you have been successful FIVE out of SEVEN DAYS in resisting the worries, you get your BIG reward!

What I Do After Week Four: Keep on going! Print out as many of the weekly goal sheets as you like, and work on *gradually* upping your resist goal. Remember, learning to resist worrying is not a race. It is a process that necessitates practice, perseverance and intestinal fortitude.

My Resistance Forms!

WEEK ONE

If you resist worrying at least one time each day, you get your small daily reward!

SUNDAY DATE: _____

- Make a tally mark for each time you resist: _____

- I resisted _____ time(s) today.

- I got my reward, which was:_____!

MONDAY DATE: _____

- Make a tally mark for each time you resist: _____

- I resisted _____ time(s) today.

- I got my reward, which was: _____!

TUESDAY DATE: _____

- Make a tally mark for each time you resist: _____

- I resisted _____ time(s) today.

- I got my reward, which was: _____!

WEDNESDAY DATE: _____

- Make a tally mark for each time you resist: _____

- I resisted _____ time(s) today.

- I got my reward, which was: _____!

THURSDAY DATE: _____

- Make a tally mark for each time you resist: _____

- I resisted _____ time(s) today.

- I got my reward, which was: _____!

FRIDAY DATE: _____

- Make a tally mark for each time you resist: _____

- I resisted _____ time(s) today.

- I got my reward, which was: _____!

SATURDAY DATE: _____

- Make a tally mark for each time you resist: _____

- I resisted _____ time(s) today.

- I got my reward, which was: _____!

Now, count up how many days you were successful (received your daily reward). If you were successful at least five of the seven days, you get your BIG reward!

- I was successful _____ days.

- My BIG reward is _____!

WEEK TWO

If you resist worrying at least one time each day, you get your small daily reward!

SUNDAY DATE: _____

- Make a tally mark for each time you resist: _____

- I resisted _____ time(s) today.

- I got my reward, which was: _____!

MONDAY DATE: _____

- Make a tally mark for each time you resist: _____

- I resisted _____ time(s) today.

- I got my reward, which was: _____!

TUESDAY DATE: _____

- Make a tally mark for each time you resist: _____

- I resisted _____ time(s) today.

- I got my reward, which was: _____!

WEDNESDAY DATE:_____

- Make a tally mark for each time you resist: _____

- I resisted _____ time(s) today.

- I got my reward, which was: _____!

THURSDAY DATE: _____

- Make a tally mark for each time you resist: _____

- I resisted _____ time(s) today.

- I got my reward, which was: _____!

FRIDAY DATE: _____

- Make a tally mark for each time you resist: _____

- I resisted _____ time(s) today.

- I got my reward, which was: _____!

SATURDAY DATE: _____

- Make a tally mark for each time you resist: _____

- I resisted _____ time(s) today.

- I got my reward, which was: _____!

Now, count up how many days you were successful (received your daily reward). If you were successful at least five of the seven days, you get your BIG reward!

- I was successful _____ days.

- My BIG reward is _____!

WEEK THREE

If you resist worrying at least two times each day, you get your small daily reward!

SUNDAY DATE: _____

- Make a tally mark for each time you resist: _____

- I resisted _____ time(s) today.

- I got my reward, which was: _____!

MONDAY DATE: _____

- Make a tally mark for each time you resist: _____

- I resisted _____ time(s) today.

- I got my reward, which was: _____!

TUESDAY DATE: _____

- Make a tally mark for each time you resist: _____

- I resisted _____ time(s) today.

- I got my reward, which was: _____!

WEDNESDAY DATE: _____

- Make a tally mark for each time you resist: _____

- I resisted _____ time(s) today.

- I got my reward, which was: _____!

THURSDAY DATE: _____

- Make a tally mark for each time you resist: _____

- I resisted _____ time(s) today.

- I got my reward, which was: _____!

FRIDAY DATE: _____

- Make a tally mark for each time you resist: _____

- I resisted _____ time(s) today.

- I got my reward, which was: _____!

SATURDAY DATE: _____

- Make a tally mark for each time you resist: _____

- I resisted _____ time(s) today.

- I got my reward, which was: _____!

Now, count up how many days you were successful (received your daily reward). If you were successful at least five of the seven days, you get your BIG reward!

- I was successful _____ days.

- My BIG reward is _____!

WEEK FOUR

If you resist worrying at least two times each day, you get your small daily reward!

SUNDAY DATE: _____

- Make a tally mark for each time you resist: _____

- I resisted _____ time(s) today.

- I got my reward, which was: _____!

MONDAY DATE: _____

- Make a tally mark for each time you resist: _____

- I resisted _____ time(s) today.

- I got my reward, which was: _____!

TUESDAY DATE: _____

- Make a tally mark for each time you resist: _____

- I resisted _____ time(s) today.

- I got my reward, which was: _____!

WEDNESDAY DATE: _____

- Make a tally mark for each time you resist: _____

- I resisted _____ time(s) today.

- I got my reward, which was: _____!

THURSDAY DATE: _____

- Make a tally mark for each time you resist: _____

- I resisted _____ time(s) today.

- I got my reward, which was: _____!

FRIDAY DATE: _____

- Make a tally mark for each time you resist: _____

- I resisted _____ time(s) today.

- I got my reward, which was: _____!

SATURDAY DATE: _____

- Make a tally mark for each time you resist: _____

- I resisted _____ time(s) today.

- I got my reward, which was: _____!

Now, count up how many days you were successful (received your daily reward). If you were successful at least five of the seven days, you get your BIG reward!

- I was successful _____ days.

- My BIG reward is _____!

WEEK _____

If I resist worrying at least ____ times each day, I get my small daily reward!

SUNDAY DATE: _____

- Make a tally mark for each time you resist: _____

- I resisted _____ time(s) today.

- I got my reward, which was: _____!

MONDAY DATE: _____

- Make a tally mark for each time you resist: _____

- I resisted _____ time(s) today.

- I got my reward, which was: _____!

TUESDAY DATE: _____

- Make a tally mark for each time you resist: _____

- I resisted _____ time(s) today.

- I got my reward, which was: _____!

WEDNESDAY DATE: _____

- Make a tally mark for each time you resist: _____

- I resisted _____ time(s) today.

- I got my reward, which was: _____!

THURSDAY DATE: _____

- Make a tally mark for each time you resist: _____

- I resisted _____ time(s) today.

- I got my reward, which was: _____!

FRIDAY DATE: _____

- Make a tally mark for each time you resist: _____

- I resisted _____ time(s) today.

- I got my reward, which was: _____!

SATURDAY DATE: _____

- Make a tally mark for each time you resist: _____

- I resisted _____ time(s) today.

- I got my reward, which was: _____!

Now, count up how many days you were successful (received your daily reward). If you were successful at least five of the seven days, you get your BIG reward!

I was successful _____ days.

My BIG reward is _____!

Take Life One Bite at a Time

Notice that this book is not written in one long paragraph. If it were, you would never read it. The read would just be way too overwhelming. Typically, however, most of us approach life as if it were one long paragraph, and feel completely overwhelmed by it.

Question: How do you eat an elephant?

Answer: One bite at a time.

When we wake up in the morning, we might think about all the things we have to do or complete, and then that we'll never get them all done. This leads to a feeling of anxiety and dread, and, yes, eventually depression. You feel tired (and so not fab) before you even get out of the bed.

Bite it!

Instead of overwhelming ourselves with a long, never-ending list, each day should be thought of in bites. Your day should NOT *only* be looked at as what it is that you NEED TO BE DOING every hour of the day, but also in regard to WHAT YOU HAVE DONE. It is necessary to realize the little things you have accomplished with your day. Each moment has counted for you in some way, and seeing the benefit of even minor interactions and activities is of utmost importance.

Realizing what you have done with your day keeps you from saying "I got nothing accomplished today." This is referred to as "All or Nothing Thinking." It does you no good to think, "I didn't get everything accomplished today, so basically my day was wasted." Plus, this is simply not true.

Sometimes, your body is telling you that you need a rest. I call these "Spa Days." If you take a day to rejuvenate yourself, whether through watching some TV, taking a bath, or reading a book, enjoy it! Realize that you are taking a Spa Day, and label it so. DO NOT take the Spa Day then beat yourself up over not having accomplished anything during your special Spa Day time. What you did accomplish, what you bit off that day, was much needed "R and R" (aka "Rest and Relaxation").

Does this mean that you should spend every day in bed? No. But consider whether you're doing something destructive in your life that needs to stop, because it's depleting your ability to function every day. If giving up and not getting up is an issue for you, you *do* need to focus on getting some help to get going!

OTHERWISE:

- Remember, BIG things get taken care of by taking little bites.

- It is important to realize that everything you do during the day counts as a little bite, whether it's part of a bigger project or not.

- Appreciate the BIGGER and smaller things that happen during the day.

- Getting little bites accomplished is better than getting no bites accomplished.

- Glean enjoyment from the activity at hand.

- It is easier to experience enjoyment of everyday activities when you are in the Here and Now (the section on the Here and Now—"Just Pet the Dog"—is coming up soon!).

- Appreciating little bites of life allows you to not be uber focused on just completing tasks.

- It is important to realize that each bite of the elephant counts.

Little (and BIG) Bites

These things count as bites:

- Taking the time to call a friend

- Gardening

- Taking a bubble bath

- Reading a book

- Organizing photos

- Doing some work

- Doing a *lot* of work

- A home-cooked meal

- Taking a nap

Put your other "bite ideas" below:

- _____

- _____

- _____

- _____

- _____

Take Life One Bite at a Time Tool

Use "MY DAY IN 'BITES'" form now, to practice taking your day in bites. Then, once you've had practice taking your day one bite at a time, keep this log as your "go to tool" when you start to feel overwhelmed.

Under the "Bite Off a Piece" column, write the amount of time you spent in your activity. Then, list your activity under the "Activity" column.

Next, write in the aspect that you enjoyed or gained from that activity.

This will lead to recording what you learned from the activity, whether it be positive or negative.

If you had a negative experience, write what it was you learned. If you have difficulty with this particular aspect of the exercise, then start your sentence with this: "Next time I will _____." For example, you could say, "Next time I will trust my instincts and not confide in someone when my flag goes up," or "Next time I will say 'no,'" or "Next time I will bring an umbrella." Once you have practiced saying "Next time I will _____," start saying, "What I learned from this experience was_____." Then put the fact that you learned something in your Fab Good Stuff folder. Bonus!

Sometimes it takes quite a bit of practice to start phrasing regrets in your brain as learning experiences. Use this next page to help remind you to *learn*, instead of *yearn*!

You can even color in the "bites" on the table to reflect how you felt during that "bite" of your day!

As you are going through the day, or at the end of the day, look over your "MY DAY IN 'BITES'" page. Say out loud, "Man, I'm a fabulous animal! Look at all of these bites I took today!"

My Day in "Bites" Form

Date:_____

Bite Off a Piece!	Activity	What I Enjoyed/Gained	What I Learned
Time:			
Time:			
Time:			
Time:			
Time:			
Time:			
Time:			
Time:			
Time:			
Time:			
Time:			
Time:			
Time:			
Time:			
Time:			
Time:			
Time:			
Time:			
Time:			
Time:			
Time:			
Time:			
Time:			

Give Yourself a "T!"

You're WONDERFUL!

You have completed DAY FIVE!

Give yourself a

Get ready for gorgeous:

DAY 6

Shelf Life

There are some negative things that have happened in your life that you will not forget. That's okay. Having the expectation that you will forget everything negative that ever happened to you is not realistic. Unfortunately, people are often so desperate to forget the negative things in their lives that they use an excessive amount of energy avoiding the negative thoughts in their minds. It is as if there is a mini-me running around in the brain, trying to not look at or think about the negative experiences sitting there. Sometimes, folks spend so much time and energy trying to ignore the big fat negatives in their brain that they are exhausted.

Here's a fact. Being exhausted saps your *happy energy* right away. Does it take energy to be happy? Of course! Does it take energy to be fabulous? Of course! Is HAPPY automatic? No! Is FABULOUS automatic? No! You can't work on the happiness/fabulous project in your brain if you are too pooped from jogging around the icky stuff all day.

So put the icky in the box, put the top on the box, and stick the box on a shelf in your brain where it is out of the way!

Now we have the icky stuff where it belongs. But what about the little gems that have happened in your life? Those need to be brought out more frequently. People tend to be all too ready to open the Icky Box, but ignore the pretty box with a bow—the Gems Box—that has the funny, silly, happy moments. Put the things in the Gems Box like an achievement you've reached, pride for your kid, a joke on TV that made you laugh, the sound of rain on a cozy day, or the feeling of the sunshine and birds twittering on a bright day. Your own personal gems in your pretty box can be anything, and they do not have to be big things. In fact, you will collect more gems if they include little things!

Why is it so tempting to repeatedly open the Icky Box and ignore the Gems Box? We have already talked about how people have a tendency to think more about things that are cognitively dissonant. If you have two or more opposing thoughts in your mind, you feel pressured to resolve that inconsistency because unresolved thoughts make you feel uncomfortable. And the things that do not make sense to us tend to lead to very bothersome thoughts. We feel that we need to resolve the conflicting thoughts, so we think about them more. However, when we think about negative things more than the positive things, it can change our perspective to one of negativity. For example, there is a concept related to cognitive dissonance called the Zeigarnik Effect. With the Zeigarnik Effect, we tend to remember an uncompleted task more than a task that we have completed. Many times, people tend to overestimate how poorly they did on a test. They are focusing more on the questions to which they did *not* know the answer, or did not correctly complete, as opposed to the questions to which they *did* know the answer. As a result, the person leaves the test ruminating about the answers that he or she did not know. This colors the person's entire perspective about how they did on the test. They feel that they performed much more poorly, overall.

Do not let focusing on the negative Icky Box color your entire perspective on life. Choose your outlook by choosing to take a peek at the Gems Box much more frequently!

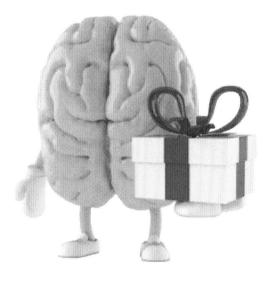

Shelf Life Tool

Place your negative thought in a box in your brain, so to speak, put the top on it, and place that Icky Box on a shelf in your brain. Make sure the shelf is out of the way in some corner. When you need to look at that negative thought for some reason, you can take the box off the shelf and remove the lid. Just do not forget to put the negative thought back in the box again when you are finished with it!

Remember, grab your Gems Box frequently! Choose fabulous by choosing to look at your Gems as often as possible!

GEMS BOX—STUFF I NEED TO LOOK AT OFTEN

1._____

2._____

3._____

4._____

5._____

ICKY BOX—STUFF I NEED TO SHELVE

1._____

2._____

3._____

4._____

Goal Setting

Set your goals with acute attention to priorities. Everyone should have one priority every day that needs to happen, no matter what. There is no way that you are going to accomplish everything you think you need to do in one day. But there's probably one thing that you feel absolutely has to happen.

I have heard many people lament that they are depressed because they just did not get enough accomplished in a day. But feeling overwhelmed is a recipe for a tanking mood. Feeling overwhelmed is funk-producing.

Having too much to do will do nothing but bury you in guilt that those things did not happen. This buries your fabulousness. Every day, ONE goal or activity is important for you to accomplish. It is up to you to decide what that priority is. You must have a Plan A Goal, then a Plan B Goal if you happen to have enough time. If the stars are aligned for you, you might, and I mean *might*, get a Plan C Goal accomplished. Your Plan A Goal might be to get to work. If you have to work during the day, getting to work and doing your best is your first priority. As long as that happens, you had a successful day.

Next, you are allowed to have a second goal during the day. Your Plan B Goal might be to clean the house. However, if that goal is not accomplished, you do not have a license to beat yourself up about it. That is your bonus goal. If you have the energy left over, or the time, Plan B Goal is the second thing you do. Maybe Plan B Goal is to make dinner. If you are too exhausted to go grocery shopping after work, and picked up fast food instead, oh well. No big deal. Going grocery shopping after work was your Plan B Goal. Just put grocery shopping as your Plan A Goal on Saturday. Of course, then make sure that you go grocery shopping for the week on Saturday. That way, you do not need to list it as a goal for another week or two.

Finally, you can even have a third task that you would like to accomplish. Again, if you do not accomplish this goal you are not allowed to self-flagellate. Plan C Goal may be to work on an extra project, like a blog, or to shop for a gift for someone. If it does not happen, erase that goal and rewrite it on a day when you won't be so overwhelmed.

Let me be clear. If you get Plan A Goal accomplished, you have had a successful day. Pat yourself on the back. If Plan B Goal happens, do a happy dance. If Plan C Goal occurs, do not expect it to happen daily, but you have 100 percent permission to have the Plan C Goal Glow for the next five days.

When you meet a goal, do a happy dance!

Goal Setting Tool

List your goals by the day. Notice that the spaces for your goals are not very big. There is a reason for this. Just list your goals A, B, and C simply and briefly. And list them in pencil. If you do not accomplish a goal for the day, do not beat yourself up. Erase it and put it on the next day. That is the reason erasers were invented!

Week of: _____

	Sun.	Mon.	Tues.	Wed.	Thurs.	Fri.	Sat.
Plan A Goal							
Plan B Goal							
Plan C Goal							

Give Yourself an "O!"

STUPENDOUS!

You have completed DAY SIX!

Give yourself an

Now slide into sensational:

DAY 7

A Hopeless Realist

It has been said that those with depression are just realists. They actually see the world and future as it is, which causes them to be depressed. I cannot imagine the reason for this philosophy. Saying that you are a "realist," which you believe justifies your depression, keeps you "realists" with depression "stuck." These "realists" are the best "Yes butters" ever.

Ok, "realists," hang onto your seats. Here's the news flash: You are not enough of a realist. That's right. You are not doing a good enough job at your job of being a realist. True realists understand that there is evidence of the unexplainable. Most of life is unexplainable. Hope is one alternative to looking at the future. By discounting the existence of hope and possibility, you are discounting something very real. Change is always possible, no matter how many barriers you set up for yourself. It is all about CHOICES. CHOOSE to think negatively and try to fool yourself into thinking you are being a realist, or CHOOSE to affect change within yourself and your life by taking a big bite of the apple of HOPE. CHOOSE to be UNREAL. CHOOSE to be FABULOUS!

A Hopeless Realist Tool

Say this out loud every day: "Hope, possibility, change." Then believe it.

If you are having a negative thought, one way to distract yourself is to say these words aloud. Do it in front of a mirror. Smile and wink at yourself. Then say, "I'm pretty fabulous!"

Everything Is an Activity

Hanging with Others

So often, we discount interacting with other people as an activity. We think that it's actually wasting time. We believe that the only things that count as "productive" are those centered around work. Well, having a conversation with someone is an activity that counts. Talking to your mother on the phone, or your child about his or her day is an activity. It fills your cup. Human connections are things you will remember. Make time for them.

Chilling on Your Own—Carpe Diem!

Additionally, relaxing is, and should be considered, an activity. This afternoon, my husband said, "Wow, it's already two o'clock! Where did the day go?" This shows that he felt as if he had not been productive enough, and that the entire day to that point had been a waste. I pointed out that our morning activity had been relaxing. Again, it counts.

One evening, my daughter was helping me bring items inside from the car, but told me she would be inside shortly. As I was rushing inside, I turned to see what was taking her so long. She had calmly stopped after getting out of the car to take pictures of the fading rays of the sun coming through the clouds. She was taking life by the hand and dancing with it, while I was focused on rushing to my next task. Life lessons truly happen every day, and we can learn from those around us—younger, older, or in-between.

CARPE DIEM! SIEZE THE DAY!

Everything Is an Activity Tool

In your "Relax Me Some Quality!" log, write down a time every day that you will spend relaxing for at least five minutes. Plan and document quality time that you will spend with someone each day. If you do not plan this in advance, but it just happens, that's great! You can document a summary of your interaction in your log, then refer back to all of the fabulously cool times you had hanging out with people (or relaxing on your own) when you need some Brain Candy! List your week's favorites!

(Hint: You can have more than one favorite a week, just like you can have lots of best fab friends!)

Relax Me Some Quality!

Week's Date:_____

SUNDAY
I will relax at (time: _____).

My relaxation activity will be _____.

My quality time experience will be with _____.

What we did was _____.

MONDAY
I will relax at (time: _____).

My relaxation activity will be _____.

My quality time experience will be with _____.

What we did was _____.

TUESDAY

I will relax at (time: _____).

My relaxation activity will be _____.

My quality time experience will be with _____.

What we did was _____.

WEDNESDAY

I will relax at (time: _____).

My relaxation activity will be _____.

My quality time experience will be with _____.

What we did was _____.

THURSDAY

I will relax at (time: _____).

My relaxation activity will be _____.

My quality time experience will be with _____.

What we did was _____.

FRIDAY

I will relax at (time: _____).

My relaxation activity will be _____.

My quality time experience will be with _____.

What we did was _____.

SATURDAY

I will relax at (time: _____).

My relaxation activity will be _____.

My quality time experience will be with _____.

What we did was _____.

Celebrate!

Celebrate some of your top experiences of the week!

Week of: _____.

Write the name of your fab friend, insert a pic of that person or you with that person, draw a pic of that person, or make a collage of a bunch of experiences. It's up to you!

Give Yourself an "F!"

You're BRILLIANT!

You have completed DAY SEVEN!

Give yourself an

Now fall into phenomenal:

DAY 8

Just Pet the Dog

It is impossible to focus on the *here and now* when you're worrying. Worry is usually focused on the past or the future. John Lennon wrote, "Life is what happens to you while you're busy making other plans." I like to take a twist on this, and say, "Life is what happens when you're busy thinking about something else." Like thinking about something else you need to be doing while life is going on right in front of you. You are missing life because you are too caught up in ruminating about the past or worrying about the future. When your brain is negatively in the past or the future, you are basically worrying about and focusing on the funk. Think about how much life you are missing when you are not in the *here and now*!

One good strategy to use in order to avoid thinking about the funk and focusing on the fabulous is to focus instead on what you are seeing, hearing, smelling, and feeling as often as possible. If you are outside, think about how the sun feels on your skin, the cool air on your cheek, and the ground beneath your feet. When we come home after a hard day, many of us walk in the door distracted. While we are petting the dog, we think about the negative things that happened during the day, what we need to make for dinner, and whether or not the kids have finished their homework (or whether or not we have done our homework, for that matter, if we are going to school). We are not thinking about that dog's beautiful eyes or how nice the fur feels under our hands. We are not focused on the fact that we are so lucky to have such a wonderful animal in our lives. Four or five other issues are playing in our minds, cluttering our brain with frenetic future activities.

The enjoyment that will come to you when you make the effort to be in the here and now is FREEING. The next time you come home from work, don't let life happen while you're busy thinking about something else. Do not think about other things while you are petting the dog. Just pet the dog.

Just Pet the Dog Tool

Practice being in the "here and now" for five minutes every day. Write your observations in your "Here and Now Tool"— the things you perceive when you are in the here and now:

- What do I see?

- How does it feel?

- How does it taste?

- How does it smell?

- How does it sound?

Focusing on what your senses are picking up will help you improve your ability to be in the Here and Now.

Remember: Just Pet the Dog!

Here and Now Tool

Week's Date:_____

DAY 1

What do I see?

How does it feel?

How does it taste?

How does it smell?

How does it sound?

DAY 2

What do I see?

How does it feel?

How does it taste?

How does it smell?

How does it sound?

DAY 3

What do I see?

How does it feel?

How does it taste?

How does it smell?

How does it sound?

DAY 4

What do I see?

How does it feel?

How does it taste?

How does it smell?

How does it sound?

DAY 5

What do I see?

How does it feel?

How does it taste?

How does it smell?

How does it sound?

DAY 6

What do I see?

How does it feel?

How does it taste?

How does it smell?

How does it sound?

DAY 7

What do I see?

How does it feel?

How does it taste?

How does it smell?

How does it sound?

Brain Heels and Feather Boas

When I was doing a virtual session with a college student, she showed me a pair of heels that she had been trying on for an upcoming event. She had to decide between two of them, and put them on to show me. As she walked around in the heels, she had that look that so many women get when they put on heels, or shoes that they like. She smiled. Her posture was better. She held her head a little higher. I realized that putting on those heels made her mentally go to a different place she rarely visited; a place of positivity and feeling good about herself. Going into that zone for even a moment boosted her happiness factor. And with that, the concept of "Brain Heels" was born.

Brain heels are best described as "all that-ness." As in, "You are all that and a bag of chips." Most folks get a good feeling when they don something they like, they feel good in, or that is a little special. It's an item that helps to give a mental pick-me-up. My mother used to say she knew if I liked an article of clothing that I tried on for her because I would do a little dance when modeling it. And I didn't even realize it! But when I wear something I like, I apparently shimmy. Truth, you can't shimmy without being happy.

Sometimes it's difficult to get out of a funk when you can't imagine the fabulous. Putting on a pair of your best heels and taking a quick stroll can remind you what fabulous feels like. Even if you do not wear high heels, there is likely some article of clothing that brings out your feelings of "all that-ness."

Once you're aware of that fabulous feeling you get from your heels (or other all that-ness item), memorize it. Then, even though you are not in a position to actually put on heels and walk around, you can slip into those high heels in your brain and feel that all that-ness feeling! A cognitive shift to a different and brighter way of thinking, for even a moment, is beneficial. It battles the funk, and reminds you of the happiness for which you are striving!

Another Positivity Prop to try is a feather boa. Who doesn't like a good feather boa I ask you? It's difficult to put on a feather boa and not feel a little more fabulous. So, keep a feather boa handy. Every once in a while, go put it on and look in the mirror. Make fabulous faces at yourself. Strut around with it. Shake and shimmy. You can even grab your high heels or other all that-ness item and put those on, too!

The nice thing about your Brain Heels and your Boa is that they are always available in your mind when you need them. For example, if you're feeling a little low in the believing in yourself department before a meeting, imagine yourself putting on those heels and wrapping the boa around your neck beforehand. You'll dominate with your Brain Heels attitude, confidence, and all that-ness!

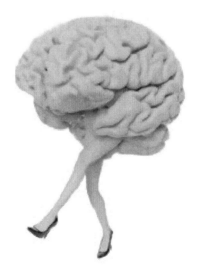

Brain Heels and Feather Boas Tool

PICK A PROP!

Pick your Positivity Prop. Your Positivity Prop is an item that immediately pulls you up into a brighter mood when you wear it. The only requirement is that you must strut around after donning your prop. If your prop is not readily available, just pretend to put it on! The perfect Positivity Prop helps you achieve the "all that-ness" feeling. Then, memorize what it feels like to be in that positive space, and return to it as often as possible. Here are some ideas for your Positivity Props:

High heels
Feather boa
Crazy boxer shorts
Wild socks
Awesome hat
Lightsaber

Next, you will list your favorite Positivity Props. You can use anything that inspires strutting, dancing, and posing!

My Most Fabulous
Positivity Props

MY MOST FABULOUS POSITIVITY PROPS:

_____

_____

_____

_____

_____

Now USE your Positivity Props whenever you need a pick me up or confidence. Cognitive shifts are good for your brain and your attitude!

Give Yourself an "A!"

You're INCREDIBLE!

You have completed DAY EIGHT!

Give yourself an

Now ease into divine:

DAY 9

King (or Queen) of Denial: Defense Mechanisms

Entire books have been written on Freudian defense mechanisms. Defense mechanisms, however, are not the emphasis of *this* book. But I will make the comment that sometimes defense mechanisms get people through extraordinarily difficult times. Here I will focus on two defense mechanisms most popular with people fond of negative and irrational thinking.

Denial

One defense mechanism is denial. If you have huge problems, thinking of the possible extent of them is not necessarily a positive thing. Thus, denial can be used to your advantage, as long as it is not permitted to run out of control. I have had severe juvenile rheumatoid arthritis since age twelve, and if I were to think about this disease all of the time, the health implications, and my future, I would not get anything accomplished during the day. I probably would not have gone to school to become a doctor. Not thinking about the disease all of the time, or in essence using the defense mechanism of denial here and there, served in my favor.

However, any defense mechanism such as denial can be damaging if taken to the extreme. If I were to completely deny the fact that I have rheumatoid arthritis, I would never go to the rheumatologist or other specialists. That would be harmful. Often, college students feel weird, stigmatized, and abnormal needing to manage their diabetes around other college students, so they stop using their treatment out of denial. The results are disastrous.

Being in DENIAL about having diabetes to the extent that one does not take insulin or other treatments can have life-ending results. This is an extreme, but real, example of the possibly damaging consequences of denial. But remember that denial can creep into your life unannounced, especially when you don't want to confront something that you probably should address. Be aware of your defense mechanisms. Where denial is concerned, "a little dab will do ya."

Don't rest on your laurels and be a King or Queen of Denial!

Rationalization

Another often-used defense mechanism is rationalization. Rationalization is a defense mechanism that justifies maladaptive behaviors. It might keep you wearing that bathrobe with all of the holes in it, or keep you in your funk because you are comfortable with it. In these cases, a rationalization for not changing might include, "Things are really okay the way that they are. I don't need to change." Rationalization could also keep you from using the tools in this book. You may think, "I don't have time for them," or "I'll look at that book later."

When working with inmates, I have often run across rationalization. For example, in order to rationalize breaking into a car and stealing something, I have heard inmates say that thefts were the victims' fault, because valuable items were visible on the front seat. The inmates who use rationalization as a defense mechanism of their stealing behaviors mentally justify their illegal activities. People with addictions will often rationalize stealing at the time that they take money by telling themselves that they will pay the money back.

It is important to realize when you are rationalizing and it is not in your best interest. For example, a maladaptive thought for you may be rationalizing not using the tools in this book by thinking that you do not have the time for them. Goal setting and paying attention to your priorities will do more to serve you in regard to getting the key things in your day accomplished, as opposed to choosing not to do what you need for yourself and using rationalizing as a defense mechanism.

Remember, you and your welfare are important, too. Take the time for yourself and keep using your *Funk to Fabulous* tools. Checking out Funktofabulous.com may also be helpful. Unless your funk is under control, you won't be able to meet the other goals in your life. Don't rationalize fabulous away!

King (or Queen) of Denial: Defense Mechanisms Tool

Here is a crown for you! Print as many as you need to fit around your head, cut them out, and tape them together. Or, use your own favorite crown you just might happen to have lying around! Every time you use denial, put your crown on. The key is to be aware of when you're using a defense mechanism. If you are being the Queen (or King) of Denial, wear the crown. You can put the crown on if you are using rationalization, too. Sometimes it is fun to have a family member or buddy hand you the crown if they catch you using a defense mechanism!

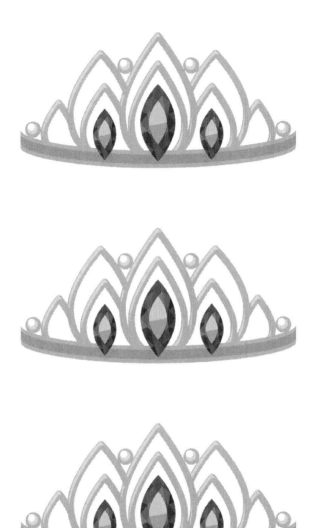

Foreground and Background: Keeping It in Perspective

Perspective

Many people have a tendency to spend the same amount of time on every worry. The person may worry that he is not a good enough son, or that he is not putting enough into work. A conversation may not go as planned, which can cause another worry. It is common for someone to begin worrying, and then obsessing, about whether or not a statement she made hurt someone's feelings.

Even if success has been realized, a person may turn the positive into a worry. For example, the student who was praised for his acting abilities may initially be elated, but then eventually think, "I don't think I was doing the best I could. What's wrong with me? I know I can do better." Younger children will sometimes worry excessively about not having followed a rule. Adults will worry about making a minor mistake at work.

Getting to the point where you realize that not every worry should be given the same attention is huge. This helps battle the funk. In art, "perspective" is the concept that things can be painted to look closer to the observer or further away. A road may start off looking wide, and then narrow at the tip to make the road look as if it is in the distance. We must paint our thoughts and concerns in much the same way. How we think about our worries, and how we organize them, is our choice. Having perspective means knowing the difference between big worries, medium worries, and little worries.

Foreground and Background: Keeping It in Perspective Tool

Perspective

CLASSIFY IT!

When you have a worry, it should be classified. You can do this by classifying the worry as big, medium, or little. Then give it the appropriate amount of time during your Worry Time. For example, if a worry is a big worry, you may spend most of your time troubleshooting it. If it is a small worry, do not allot as much time. Please note that most people tend to spend most of their time worrying about the little worries, viewing them erroneously as big worries. Be careful that this does not happen to you! This mistake brings on the funk!

TILE IT!

Another tool that helps keep things "in perspective" is a physical number line. If you have tile in your house, count off ten tiles in a line. The starting tile is for your smallest worry. The farthest tile is for the biggest worry possible. If you do not have tile, then place pieces of construction paper, with different colors if you have them, in a line.

Next, pick the "smallest worry" tile and label it with the most innocuous action of which you can think. Stepping on an ant is something that most people, no matter how much they worry, do not feel is a big deal. So, if you never worry about stepping on an ant, label your closest tile with that (or an alternate action that causes you no worry). On the other far end, label the tile with premeditated murder. Yes, if you have plotted the murder of someone, then that should be a cause for concern. Perhaps label the next tile down from that as stealing money from your mother's purse.

WALK THE LINE!

Now you have created two extremes. The next time you have a worry, walk your worry line. Or, you can use your "Keeping it in Perspective Scale." Pick exactly where on the line your current worry should fall. Should it be on the end toward the ant, or down toward murder? Step on the appropriate tile, and put your worry into perspective! You will likely surprise yourself with how many "ant stepping" sorts of worries you have!

Keep Your Worries in

Perspective

Keeping It in Perspective Scale

Date:_____

RATE YOUR WORRY!

| | | | | | | | | | |

Stepping on ant   Premeditated
Murder

My worry is:

BIG: _____

Medium: _____

Small: _____

RATE YOUR WORRY!

| | | | | | | | | | | |

Stepping on ant   Premeditated
                                                       Murder

My worry is:

BIG: _____

Medium: _____

Small: _____

RATE YOUR WORRY!

| | | | | | | | | | | |

Stepping on ant   Premeditated
                                                       Murder

My worry is:

BIG: _____

Medium: _____

Small: _____

Give Yourself a "B!"

You're MAGNIFICENT!

You have completed DAY NINE!

Give yourself a

Now race into rad:

DAY 10

Be a Shifter

Some of the funniest people I know have had the most difficult lives. They have usually learned to cope by looking at the world differently. People find humor in things that are presented in an offbeat or unexpected way, and taking a situation that is difficult, or a worry, and finding a way to look at it differently, may help you see the humor in a situation. Clearly, this does not work for tragedies. However, for the day-to-day strife that occurs in life, a little humor can be helpful.

Looking at something in a completely different way is called a "cognitive shift." Sometimes it is difficult to get through a funk because we are so bogged down in our thinking that we just cannot see it a different way. We are unable to shift.

Be the unexpected! See the funny side of life!

I have mentioned having juvenile rheumatoid arthritis. This is a degenerative inflammatory process that causes mechanical changes in the joints. So, many joints of people with RA look different. My husband has an interesting perspective on my toes, which are decidedly not straight. He does not say that my toes are bent; they just happen to have a very poor sense of direction. He has thus labeled them as "directionally confused!" This is a cognitive shift about my toes which is funny and shows that Kevin finds them endearing at the same time.

Comedians have honed their brains to look at almost every situation with a flexible mind. They cognitively shift everyday occurrences so that they can see many different perspectives. Comedian Jerry Seinfeld said, "I don't understand how a woman can take boiling hot wax, pour it on her upper thighs, rip the hair out by the roots, and still be afraid of a spider." By saying the unexpected and looking at situations a different way, we all get a laugh, and see the "funny" side of life. Always remember, laughing is fabulous!

Be a Shifter Tool

Catch yourself with worries as they occur, and make a cognitive shift by looking at something in a different way with some humor. This will help keep you from becoming so engrained in your negative thinking and funk that it is difficult to see another perspective. Don't take yourself or your worries too seriously!

SHIFTER SHEET

My worry is:

_____.

A completely different way to think about my worry is:

_____.

Now laugh! (or chuckle or snicker)!

My worry is:

_____.

A completely different way to think about my worry is:

_____.

Now laugh! (or guffaw or giggle)!

My worry is:

_____.

A completely different way to think about my worry is:

_____.

Now laugh! (or chortle or hohoho)!

Keep your "Shifter Sheet" handy and return to it when you have problems making your cognitive shift. You can help remind yourself how you have shifted to the funny before!

Roll with the Punches

It's not only our thinking that can be different, but our behavior as well, because they are linked. Sometimes we begin thinking differently to change our behavior, and sometimes we change our behavior to begin thinking differently. You can *choose* a different behavioral reaction. A more positive one. For example, if your car alarm accidentally goes off, you can choose to become agitated and irritated and angry. You will frown as a result. Or, you can choose to laugh at the car alarm going off. It is an inconsequential, ridiculous thing, after all. If that's the worst thing that happens to you during the day, you will have had a pretty good day, after all!

When the car alarm is initially accidentally triggered, you might notice an automatic irritation. However, if you immediately change your frowning behavior, and laugh, this can help lead to a more positive and appropriate emotion about the silly thing. Voila! You go from funk to fabulous! You change your behavior to help change your mood!

Roll with the Punches Tool

Look at the thing that irritated you, the irritant, and choose to act differently in response to it. Instead of automatically reacting, *choose* your reaction. Try to change your facial expression in the moment, and let a more positive behavior change follow. If the moment catches you off guard, and you don't change it immediately, plot out the change with your "Roll with Those Punches! Sheet." Even though you were not successful in acting how you may have wanted at the moment, you can basically practice on paper to help you act differently next time!

Remember, you hold the power. You can change your reaction at any time. Even in the middle of being mad, you can start laughing if you like. You'll keep people wondering!

Roll with Those Punches! Sheet

DATE: _____

My irritant is/was:

_____.

The way I reacted:

I reacted the way I wanted: Yes No

(If no) A completely different way to act about my

irritant is:_____.

My irritant is/was:

_____.

The way I reacted:

I reacted the way I wanted: Yes No

(If no) A completely different way to act about my

irritant is:_____.

My irritant is/was:

_____.

The way I reacted:

I reacted the way I wanted: Yes No

(If no) A completely different way to act about my

irritant is:_____.

My irritant is/was:

_____.

The way I reacted:

I reacted the way I wanted: Yes No

(If no) A completely different way to act about my

irritant is:_____.

My irritant is/was:

_____.

The way I reacted:

I reacted the way I wanted: Yes No

(If no) A completely different way to act about my

irritant is:_____.

Be with People Who Bring You Up, Not Down

Sometimes a thinking change comes with an environmental change. I have heard love defined as the state of loving who you are when you are around a particular person. I do not know that I entirely agree with this, but there is undoubtedly truth in that different parts of us are brought out when we are around certain individuals. We may love being with certain people, but not entirely know the reason why. When we look at this, we realize that, for whatever reason, we tend to present some of the best aspects of ourselves when we are around that person. We might find that we are funnier, or nicer, or calmer when hanging out with a particular friend.

Conversely, when around other people, we may not feel as good about ourselves. The other person may be critical of you. She may misinterpret what you say, and then blame you if she is upset. You may not laugh or smile as much.

Why, then, would we spend our time with such folks? Being around people who bring out the more negative side of ourselves, or are critical of us, can reinforce that small internal voice of doubt that each of us has. No one is 100 percent sure of themselves. Everyone deals with at least some measure of self-doubt. We arm ourselves with good coping mechanisms and the hearty life we have created to attempt to make it through our days as positively as possible. When people grow up with criticism, they may be more prone to believe the disapproval thrown at them by others. And it might be complex to identify negative influences because that critical "friend" is usually not always fault-finding. Sometimes that downer, funk-producing pal you hang out with can be fun, so it can be difficult to pinpoint the negativity. We may also feel sorry for the "downers" in our lives and continue to hang out with them.

It is important to realize that you, too, are important. How you feel is important. You can create positive feelings by hanging out with people who tend to reinforce you feeling good about who you are. So, don't just sit there! Go call a positive friend!!! Being with someone who lifts you up increases your fabulousness factor! And make sure that you are being a positive friend back to them, as well! You can help increase their fabulous factor in return!

Be with People Who Bring You Up, Not Down Tool

Do not discount the health benefits of hanging out with the positive people in your life. Figure out if you have any "downers" to whom you keep exposing yourself. There may not be a need to excise them from your life completely. Just increase your positive associations. Minimize the negative. Be around people who bring you up, not down. Choose to feel better by being around the positive people and believing them! And don't be afraid to ask that optimistic person to tell you something good about yourself. Tell them awesome things about who they are, too. We often have great thoughts about other people that we do not think to share—and those thoughts might help the other person!

Use your cool tools like "Positive Person Prose," "Make a Fab Friend Day," "Fab Friend Notes," and "Fab Friend Pact" to have a positive impact on yourself and others!

Positive Person Prose

A positive person in my life is:

_____.

Here is a picture of that person (draw or paste a pic):

I believe it when that person tells me:

_____.

Repeat the above process each time you find a positive person with cool stuff to say about
you! You can even do it in your head! But writing it down can be fun, too!

Make a Fab Friend Day

Take a day to call, text, or email your Fab Friends and tell them that they are special to you. Give them the title of "Fab Friend." And you can make a "Fab Friend Pact." Here are some sample notes and pact—or make up your own!

Fab Friend Notes:

Hey, You! Just wanted you to know that you're my totally Fab Friend! You make me laugh! You are supportive, and you send me positive vibes. You know I am sending you those fabulous vibes right back! You are beautiful. I love you. I'm so lucky to have you as my Fab Friend!

OR

Hey, Fab Friend! Let's plan a day together! I'm needing some of my delicious Fab Friend time!!! I have some ideas! What do you think about: (Examples: movies, coffee, shopping, paintball, biking, running, karaoke, hiking, taking pictures, mutual hobby, baking, dancing, fishing, gardening . . .)? Now you think of some!

Ideas:

_____

_____

_____

_____

Possible Days/Times:

_____

_____

_____

_____

Being with someone who lifts you up increases your fabulousness factor!

Fab Friend Pact

Hey Fab Friend! You are so special to me that I want to make an official Fab Friend Pact with you! We are Fabulous together! So here goes:

Because you are my Fab Friend, we will hang out with or call each other regularly and be generally hilarious together. We will text each other funny pics and be supportive when need be. We will bring each other up, not down. We will think kind thoughts about each other and send positive vibes. We will not take things the wrong way or feel that we have to weigh every word we say. We will hug each other and tell each other that we are beautiful. We will love love love each other, and say so on a regular basis!

Things I love about you:

_____

_____

_____

_____

If I could give you any gift, I would close my eyes and imagine that you had:

ME: _____ YOU: _____ DATE: _____

Give Yourself a "U!"

You're SPECTACULAR!

You have completed DAY TEN!

Give yourself a

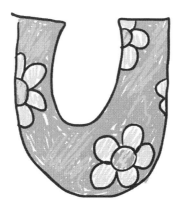

Now dance into delirious:

DAY 11

Will Exercise for Happiness

Endorphins are sometimes referred to as endogenous morphine. They are a feel-good neurotransmitter in your brain. And you also get dopamine, another happiness contributing neurotransmitter, released when the endorphins attach to your brain's reward centers. While there are even more neurotransmitters involved in happiness, we're going to focus on those beautiful endorphins.

"How do I get more of these fantastic endorphins?" you ask. The really cool thing is that you can make more endorphins on your own, without medication. All it takes is a little exercise. Exercise is a daily habit I suggest for people who are battling a case of the funks. Aerobic exercise is helpful. This can include walking, biking, running, swimming, and the like.

Exercise is not something to approach in a "Do I have time for it?" manner. It is something that you need for your health, like eating and sleeping. Being in a funk starts with your brain, but affects your whole body. You will function better with less funk and better health, so start exercising!

Remember:

Happiness is not the absence of unhappiness. Happiness takes work. It is an active sport.

Decreasing funk and increasing happiness are two different things. The expectation that once you have gotten control of your funk, happiness will automatically come, is a fallacy. Once you have worked on reducing your funk, you must concentrate on *producing* happiness. And happiness is fabulous!

Will Exercise for Happiness Tool

PICK AN EXERCISE!

Pick an exercise you feel is less distasteful than others. Or choose one that you used to love, and that misses you! Some people like going for brisk walks outside, while others enjoy riding an exercise bike while watching TV. It is helpful, if you are not a fan of exercise, to participate in exercise that is distracting. For the walkers, they usually enjoy being outside and seeing the neighborhood or nature. The exercise bike riders might enjoy watching a TV show, or reading a good book while they ride. Pick an exercise and environment that works for you!

STRUCTURE IT!

As always, structure and routine is your best friend in making a behavior change. If you are not regularly exercising now, then you will likely benefit by setting a time to exercise that fits into your life. Do not put unrealistic expectations on yourself. Planning on getting up at 5am to exercise before work, when you are a ten-time-snooze-alarm-hitting night owl, is probably not going to work. Putting a foot bike under your desk at work with an appointed time to use it every day (such as while doing paperwork) may. If you enjoy chilling in front of the TV at night, you might ride your stationary bike then.

LISTEN TO YOUR BODY!

If you have a health condition, get the exercise cleared with your doctor first. Believing you are Hercules and overdoing your exercise the first day may not be the best idea. Slow and steady wins the race. Start off realistically, with an appropriate amount of time and energy dispensed. Then, gradually increase the amount. You will eventually know the amount of time that *feels* good!

Exercise Log

I will exercise each day at _ _ : _ _ am/pm.

For my exercise, I will _____.

THIS WEEK'S DATE:_____

SUNDAY □ I exercised.	□Hated it (Did it anyway)
□ I did not exercise.	□Loved it
MONDAY □ I exercised.	□Hated it (Did it anyway)
□ I did not exercise.	□Loved it
TUESDAY □ I exercised.	□Hated it (Did it anyway)
□ I did not exercise.	□Loved it
WEDNESDAY □ I exercised.	□Hated it (Did it anyway)
□ I did not exercise.	□Loved it
THURSDAY □ I exercised.	□Hated it (Did it anyway)
□ I did not exercise.	□Loved it
FRIDAY □ I exercised.	□Hated it (Did it anyway)
□ I did not exercise.	□Loved it
SATURDAY □ I exercised.	□Hated it (Did it anyway)
□ I did not exercise.	□Loved it

And remember, don't say "I'll try."

Say, "I'll do it!"

At Least

One of the keys to being fabulous is thinking more positively. It's easy to know when we need to be more constructive in our thinking. The difficult part is knowing *how* to think more favorably about ourselves and life in general. Positive thinking is an extremely difficult construct to master. It is unrealistic to say to someone, "Just think more positively! See the glass half full!" The question is, HOW do you think more positively? How does that glass become more fabulously full?

Using specific strategies aids a change in thinking to occur. One I find effective is using the words, "At least." When a situation occurs that is frustrating, or funk-producing, we often blurt out how upset we are. Traffic may be backed up, but instead of complaining when you arrive late, saying, "Well, at least I arrived safely," reflects positive thinking. The cognition that is expressed is healthier and shows good priorities.

When I can get an entire family unit using *"at least,"* many times I see a happier family. Sometimes, I have parents use this strategy to help the children, and I start seeing more positive-thinking parents. One parent found herself using "at least" statements with her secretary. It's great when the "at least" spreads! With the use of these two little words comes a different and more positive way of thinking.

At Least Tool

Your goal is to use "at least" five times a day minimum. In the evening, you can ask your family or friends about situations in which they used an "at least." Print out and hand an "At Least Sheet" to each member of your family one morning. Tell them the "at least" plan. During the day, everyone records their "at leasts" on the sheet. Then, in the evening, everyone cuts on the dotted line and separates the "at leasts" into strips. Drop the strips into a jar. Have each family member reach into the jar and pull out a strip. Then have the person either explain (if it is their own strip they pulled) or guess (if it is someone else's strip) the situation that initially happened in order to lead to the "at least" written on the strip of paper. This not only helps spread the "at leasts" through your family, but can promote good family communication and sharing.

To get into the "at least" habit, record your "at leasts" for the first week every day. Then, when need be, you can always go back and record them for a refresher.

At Least Sheet

At least _____.

- -

At least _____.

- -

At least _____.

- -

At least _____.

- -

At least _____.

- -

At least _____.

- -

At least _____.

- -

At least _____.

- -

Give Yourself an "L!"

You're MARVELOUS!

You have completed DAY ELEVEN!

Give yourself an

Now skedaddle into scrumptious:

DAY 12

Play

Busy-itis is a severe condition known to adults and kids alike. Adults get up in the morning, rush to get ready, hurry to work, come home and take care of dinner and the kids and do more work, and fall in bed exhausted. Then they get up the next morning and do it all over again. Kids get up, rush to get ready, hurry to school, and struggle to get homework finished as quickly as possible. The thing that the kids get right is that they prioritize trying to get some fun in. The biggest problem with adults is that they have forgotten how to play.

Scheduling in fun time might seem futile. When you are a grown up, it seems that fun takes coordinating an event. It does not. Finding small things that are fun for you and that you can fit into your daily life—that's right, *daily*!—should be a priority, just like it is for kids. It does not take huge amounts of money. You may feel too tired or not motivated to have fun or play a game. Force yourself. Fun is fabulous. You will be glad you did.

I worked with a funk-ridden man who happened to be a macho type of a guy. At the end of one of our sessions, I handed him a bottle of bubbles. I thought he was going to smack me. I instructed him to blow bubbles every afternoon when he got home from work. At the next session, he expressed amazement at the bubbles. He told me he had so much fun blowing them on the back porch and watching his dog chase them. Guess who was given an extra bottle of bubbles?

Play Tool

Now it's your turn. Blow some bubbles every afternoon! You may be amazed at what happens. You also have my permission to get a children's coloring book with unicorns, Ninja Turtles, or other pages that make you smile. Indulge yourself in a new pack of crayons or colored pencils. Buy a drawing book or doodle. Play with LEGO blocks. Go to a toy store and look at the toys and games. Grab one for yourself. Playing a game with others counts, too! Get that game night going!

PLAY!

CIRCLE EACH DAY OF THE WEEK THAT YOU PLAYED.

THEN WRITE NEXT TO IT WHAT YOU DID!

Play Ideas

Some Fun & Silly & Fabulous

PLaY iDeAs

Pick up Sticks, Scrapbooking, Barbies,

Jacks, Crafts, Model Cars,

Silly String, Sand Castles, Hoola Hoops,

Hide and Seek, Blanket Fort, Nerf Ball

Coloring, Doodling, Drawing

Stickers, Bubbles, Bouncy Ball

BRAINSTORM SOME MORE

PLaY iDeAs!!!

_____	_____
_____	_____
_____	_____
_____	_____

Brain Candies

Brain candies are topics you enjoy thinking about. It is important to have positive thoughts you can rehearse in your brain to help combat the negative thoughts. In order to not just have those negative thoughts, you need to keep practicing the positive ones.

Like we discussed previously, it is easy to have negative thoughts. Unfortunately, the more accustomed your brain becomes to the negative path that worrisome thoughts travel, the more you'll tend toward negative thoughts instead of positive. When you lie awake in bed and can't sleep, your mind automatically wanders to negative thoughts. I don't think I've have ever had anyone tell me that they were so busy thinking of fun things at night that they just couldn't sleep.

Even though it may be difficult, neural pathways must be established to have positive thoughts. If associations between negative thoughts are established, and that pathway becomes well worn, you will have a tendency to think negatively. Practice is necessary if you want to stick to positive thoughts and images, which are brain candies, and develop the brain-candy pathways between your neurons.

It is okay, and even desirable, to have the same sequence of positive thoughts time and time again. After all, don't you usually have the same negative thoughts over and over again? Having the same positive thoughts repeatedly will help establish well-worn positive thought patterns. Find your delicious brain candies and think about them to your heart's content! They're calorie free!

Brain candies can be hobbies you enjoy, like playing guitar or candle making, or a funny joke you heard, a laugh you had with a friend, or a great concert you saw. Practicing thinking about these brain candies is important for creating new positive thought habits. Happiness will be experienced in short little morsels when you think about your brain candies at first, but the more you rehearse thinking those good, yummy thoughts, the more easily they will come to you!

Brain Candies Tool

Take some time to list five to ten brain candies. You can use your "Brain Candies Sheet." Then, before you go to bed at night, read over your brain candies and think about each one. Bedtime is a time of negative obsession for many. Counteract those negative funk-producing thoughts with some fabulous brain candies.

Additionally, when you decrease your worrying, you often experience what feels like brain space. Brain space is that empty area where your worries used to be. It is nice to have a list of brain candies at the ready for those times when you have been successful in decreasing your worries, but need to fill your brain space with positive thoughts!

BRAIN CANDY EXAMPLES: Hobbies like photography or soap making, singing, dancing, your pet, a day at the beach or lake, skateboarding, a funny joke you heard, fishing, surfing, a laugh you had with a friend, sunsets and sunrises, a great concert you saw or your favorite song, stickers, a cozy rainy day. . . .

Thinking of Brain Candies will help you have sweet dreams!

Brain Candies Sheet

WRITE ONE OF YOUR BRAIN CANDIES ON EACH PIECE OF CANDY.

REMEMBER TO EAT UP THOSE BRAIN CANDIES ANYTIME YOU LIKE!
BRAIN CANDIES ARE GOOD FOR YOU!

Give Yourself an "O!"

You're FANTASTIC!

You have completed DAY TWELVE!

Give yourself an

Now twist 'n' shout into tremendous:

DAY 13

Fill 'Er Up!

We often function on "empty." Our gas tank is running low, but we keep running ourselves into the ground. There are just so many demands in life. If you are not careful, those demands can drag you down into a funk. Chauffeuring the kids, errand running, activities with work, homework, relationships, the house—the list goes on and on. You can conceptualize this as a cup. Every day you should have some liquid in your cup. This liquid elixir in your cup is the stuff of which energy and positivity are made. When your cup is empty, you're in trouble. Your energy and positive mojo is lacking, and the funk can hit you more heavily. The problem is, most folks awaken, start dumping everything out of their cup with stressful activity, and do not put anything back into their cup during the day. By the afternoon, their cup is beyond empty. Folks just turn that cup over and pound on the bottom, hoping to get another drop out of it. Unfortunately, the next morning, sleep may not have been enough to add your much needed Fabulous Fluid back into your cup. It may just be empty, or near empty, when you wake up again. There may simply be nothing left to go on for the day.

Fill 'Er Up Tool

Make sure you spend as much, if not more, time putting your liquid elixir into your cup than you spend taking it out. This liquid elixir is your Fabulous Fluid. Your Fabulous Fluid will help you have energy to bring yourself up and keep yourself going.

Things that you might do to fill your cup include watching a movie, dancing, tying flies, reading a magazine, doing a relaxation technique or other mindful activity, calling a friend, or vacuuming (yes, I've had patients who love to vacuum!).

Once you start completing your daily "Cup Fillers Form," you will begin to see how little time you actually spend filling your cup. Also, you will start having to devote some brainpower to finding cool stuff you love to do. Refer to your "Cup Fillers Form" when you run out of ideas, and recycle some of your cup-filling activities! Remember, playing fills your cup, too!

Cup Fillers Form

Things I did today to fill my cup:

Goldilocks, the Science of Sleep and the Art of the Nap

The Need for Sleep

When you are rested, everything looks better. Life looks better, problems look more solvable, and colors are brighter. It is difficult to be fabulous when you are exhausted.

There is no definitive answer as to the reason we need sleep. Researchers have debated this for years. Longevity may be related to sleep. We also know that our immune systems are not as resilient if we are sleep deprived. If we are exhausted, we are more prone to illness, and may not recover as quickly if we get sick.

Keep in mind that whole tomes have and will be written that are dedicated to the elusive subject of sleep. But here is a little morsel as sleep relates to fabulousness. Hang on to your pillow!

The case as to why we need sleep may now be cracked. Here's the answer: There's just no way to feel fabulous without it! The only way to feel FABULOUS is *with* sleep! When we feel rested, we feel much more capable of taking on the world. Our mood is better. Brain function is less sluggish. When we are tired, every step can feel like an effort. Problems can feel insurmountable. Sleep puts things into perspective.

Goldilocks and the Three Bears

Sleep, at night or during a nap, is very much a Goldilocks and the Three Bears Phenomenon. Everyone feels that his or her sleep was too short, too long, or just right. The expectation for sleep to be "just right" is a lot of pressure, even for Goldilocks. Thus, number one on the priority list is to broaden our expectations of "just right." Even though we want to sleep until 9am on the weekend, awakening at 7am can be "just right" in that it allows us to enjoy more of the day. Or, we can view awakening at 5am (instead of later, as we would have preferred) as a treat, because it allows us to take in the quiet of the morning.

We can so easily view our sleep as negative if it is not "perfect." Sleep criticisms can include that we got six instead of seven hours of sleep, we did not feel exactly as refreshed as we would have liked when we awakened, it took a little longer than normal to fall asleep, or we fell asleep with our make-up on. We attach so many expectations to sleep that meeting them all is simply not going to happen.

So, first on the agenda is embracing the sleep that you *do* have. It may not be perfect, or "just right," but love the sleep you have. You can always work on tweaking it. But for now:

Don't stress out, Goldilocks! Broaden your idea of "just right."

Sleep Length

When people are in a funk, our biologic need for sleep goes into overdrive, and simply put, our brain just wants more and more sleep. Because of this, if you are in a major funk, you need to keep a log of how much you sleep in your "SLEEPY NAPPY LOG." Do not let your sleep patterns be a way of avoiding life! You still need to get going and make it through your day. Make sure you have enough sleep, but are still able to meet your daily demands. That said, if at any time you feel that you have a serious sleep disorder, you should see your doctor.

In general, documenting your sleep can help you move toward feeling more fabulous. Keep a log of your sleep in your "SLEEPY NAPPY LOG" to make sure you are getting enough. If need be, add a nap to your day in order to stretch that sleep time. Resist the urge to stay up watching your latest favorite zombie show. The light from the television can fool your brain into staying awake much longer than you should. Avoid the "I should have gotten to bed earlier hangover" the next morning.

The No Guilt Nap

Many people feel guilty about sleeping during the day. They may feel that they need a nap, but resist it. I have heard reasons ranging from "there is too much to do" to "I won't be able to fall asleep." Remember that taking a nap does not mean a marathon snooze-fest. A little sleep time during the day can be just what you need to recharge your batteries!

Some people have the fortunate gift of being able to fall asleep quickly and benefit from a fifteen-minute power nap. Others take thirty minutes to fall asleep and need two hours to feel rested. If you are dealing with a physical problem, or a chronic pain condition, you may need more sleep than the average bear. Optimal sleep may be eight hours at night with a two-hour nap during the day. Even if you cannot fall asleep, lying down and taking a load off of your entire body at once for a little while is beneficial. The time frame all depends on you—and your schedule.

Let's say you are a "rock star worker" with no time for a nap. You can optimize your nightly sleep by figuring out the times you must go to sleep at night in order to feel rested in the morning. Everyone's circadian rhythms are different. Peoples' brains naturally want to sleep and wake up at different times. If you follow these times, you can sometimes actually get away with less sleep, and still feel great. If you *must* stay up late at night, take a nap as soon as you can in the afternoon, but keep it brief. Set your alarm!

Use the "SLEEPY NAPPY LOG" to help you discover what times are best for you in regard to going to sleep at night, awakening in the morning, the length of sleep you really need, and your best nap times. Keeping track of your sleep, nap lengths and times, and how you feel during these times, can help maximize your sleep satisfaction.

While remembering that everyone is different, try this Rule of Thumb: Go to bed as early as possible, and at about the same time every night. If you awaken in the morning two hours before your alarm, go ahead and get up for the day. Going back to sleep can make you feel more tired later in the morning, when the alarm goes off.

Sweet dreams!

Sleepy Nappy Log

AWAKENING

Time: _____am/pm **Date:**_____ **Length of Sleep:** _____

Awakening was:

Automatic / With Alarm / Easy / Dreadful

Too Early / Too Late / Just Right

Emotion: Refreshed / Groggy / Exhausted / Hopeful / Happy / Fabulous / _____ (Other)

To try tomorrow: _____

NAPPING

Time: _____am/pm **Date:**_____ **Length of Nap:**_____

Napping was:

Nonexistent / Existent

Too Short / Too Long / Just Right

Emotion: Refreshed / Groggy / Exhausted / Hopeful / Happy / Fabulous / _____ (Other)

To try tomorrow: _____

FALLING ASLEEP

Time: _____am/pm **Date:**_____ **Length of Sleep:**_____

Falling Asleep was:

Automatic / Close to Target Time / Way Off Target

Easy / Dreadful / Just Right

Too Early / Too Late / Just Right

Status just prior to sleep:

Sleepy / Tired / Exhausted / Upset / Content / Happy / Hopeful / Fabulous / _____ (Other)

To try tomorrow: _____

Give Yourself a "U!"

HOORAY!

You have completed DAY THIRTEEN!

Give yourself a

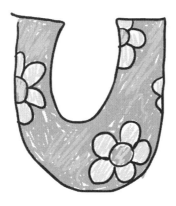

It's DAY FOURTEEN!

(Bet you're feeling tingly all over!)

DAY 14

Superheroes and Superpower Fallacy

Most people believe that superheroes are real. I'm not referring to the superheroes with X-ray vision, enhanced senses, or shape shifting abilities. Without realizing it, people often expect others to be superheroes and read their minds.

A superpower often portrayed in movies is the ability to read everyone else's thoughts. Needless to say, the people in your life cannot tap directly into your brain. However, this does not mean that they do not love you. But because they don't know everything going on in your mind, they do not always know what it is that you need or want from them.

I have often heard people say, "If he truly loved me, I would not have to tell him that I need more attention," or "If they cared, they would know what I want on my birthday," or other such nonsensical statements. People cannot read your mind. Even on a simple everyday basis people tend to not communicate exactly what they want. If you get your daughter the honey ham that you think that she loves, and she asks about the spicy pineapple ham which says is her favorite, both parties end up being bummed. Regular communication is essential! Expecting others to read your mind leads to frustration and disappointment on your part as well as others.

Let others know what you want or need from them (without being pushy, of course). No mind reading allowed. You, as well as those about whom you care, will be much happier.

Superpower Fallacy Tool

1. Don't expect others to have a mind reading superpower. You need to tell them what you want or need. Yes, this can feel weird. But it's okay to say, "I need a hug," or "I want some one-on-one time with you. Let's go out to dinner tonight." This approach will lead to many more fabulous feelings instead of waiting around and seeing if your person picks up on your need for a hug or individual time.

2. On the flip side, start asking others what you can do for them. Truly, you can't read minds, either. Sometimes, the answer may surprise you. Others may be able to better answer you if you rephrase the question. For example, if you ask a friend what would make her life easier (as opposed to what she needs) during a difficult time, she may respond, "Picking up family from the airport." That's how you get to be the real superhero!

3. You can also always do things for yourself and get yourself little treats that you want. For example, sometimes a massage, latte or even a simple smile or wink at yourself in the mirror is just what you need. And you would know. After all, you can read your own mind!

Superheroes Need a Quick Change

Try the old coin in the jar trick. Each time you tell someone what you need as opposed to expecting that person to read your mind, reward yourself with some change in a jar. You can also drop a coin in your jar for asking what others need. Then, you'll have a little nest egg to pay for treats that you might want, like that latte! Relying on the money you collect in your jar for certain goodies is an added incentive for you to tell others what you want and not expect others to have mind-reading superpowers!

I deposited ___¢ because I _____.

I deposited ___¢ because I _____.

I deposited ___¢ because I _____.

I deposited ___¢ because I _____.

I deposited ___¢ because I _____.

I deposited ___¢ because I _____.

I deposited ___¢ because I _____.

I deposited ___¢ because I _____.

I deposited ___¢ because I _____.

Q: Why do you need a jar for your change?

A: Because Superheroes don't have pockets!

Talking Heads

We are all constant talkers. If we are not talking out loud, we are continuously talking to ourselves in our heads. Even if you are the shy type who chooses words carefully, you regularly engage in self-talk. Who is always listening to you? You are!

Since you are your most consistent audience, make your self-talk, the talking to yourself in your mind, positive. If someone were to call you a loser, guilt you, and not say nice things to you, you would probably soon stop associating with that person. You will not hang out with them because they are mean to you. So don't be mean to yourself. Make your self-talk positive.

It can be challenging to get rid of negative statements that are on repeat in your brain. Sometimes that internal voice is someone else's who was not kind to you at some point in your life. In this case, that yucky voicemail left in your brain must be erased or at least placed in the Icky Box.

No replaying negative tapes or voicemails in your brain!

There is probably at least one person in your life who left words of encouragement and wisdom in your brain. Those are the internal voicemails that must be found and replayed. At times, we ignore those positive voicemails and purposefully attempt to motivate ourselves through negative self-talk. That must change. Rewards increase behavior, so rewarding yourself through positive self-talk will get you further toward meeting your goals. You will naturally engage in more positive behaviors by encouraging yourself through positive self-talk. Be a running commentary of *positive* statements to yourself rather than negative ones.

Talking Heads Tool

Catch yourself being a bad talking head. Replace those downer, funk-producing thoughts about yourself with fabulous-producing thoughts to build yourself up!

Each time you speak badly about yourself in your own head ("I'm a loser, I'm stupid, I failed"), circle a sad head. Each time you replace that negative thought with a positive thought about yourself ("I'm pretty cool!" or "I rock!" and "Good for me!"), circle a star. Challenge yourself to get more stars than sad heads!

Positive Thinking Phrases

I'm pretty cool!

I rock!

Good for me!

That was awesome!

Incredible!

Wow!

Go me! Go me!

Amazing!

Now it's your turn to add some Positive Thinking Phrases!

_____

_____

_____

_____

Stars!

Remember, get those stars!

DAY: _____

DAY: _____

DAY: _____

DAY: _____

DAY: _____

DAY: _____

DAY: _____

Give Yourself an "S!"

You're FABULOUS!

You're FANTABULOUS!!!

You have completed DAY FOURTEEN!

Give yourself an

Woohoo!!!

Fab Celebration

Fab CELEBRATION!!!

You made it through the fourteen days! You're FABULOUS! Woohoo!!! Do a happy dance! Jump around and yell, "I did it!" Sing an "I did it!!" song. You made it! You rock! Look at all that you've accomplished! You are truly awe-inspiring!

PICS OF ME JUMPING AROUND:

Use the Funk to Fabulous Tool Belt!

Now get your soap that we talked about on Day One. The time has come! Can you believe it? You get to write, "I've gone from FUNK to FABULOUS!"

To keep up your fabulousness, continue using those fantabulous tools you've picked up over the last fourteen days! Your *Funk to Fabulous* Tools contain the nuts and bolts of what you need for daily fabulousness. *Funk to Fabulous* is intended to use over and over. Do not keep this book pretty! Love it! Use it until it falls apart!

You may forget some of your tools. NO!!!! Go to Funktofabulous.com for helpful content to keep you on course with your fabulousness!

And keep *Funk to Fabulous* out and handy. Flip through it frequently, and rediscover tools you may have forgotten. When you notice yourself getting down-in-the-dumpolas and in a funk, pull it out and give it a thorough re-read for a refresher course!

Remember, it's all good, and if it's not, we're gonna make it that way!

And never forget that you're FABULOUS!

Happy Tool Belting!

BIG Love and Hugs,

Dr. Mary

Acknowledgments

Thank you to my amazing patients. They inspire me every day with their courage to take on life in the face of immense challenges. I am grateful to take that journey with you and happy that we get to laugh a little along the way!

Growing up, I was fortunate to have the influence of many in my family who were great examples of happiness, even though they had imperfect lives.

Thank you to my mother, Martha, who sacrificed so much for her children and still gave others untold joy through her incredible vocal performances. She saw the world through different eyes. My approach to life is largely shaped by her unique perspective. Martha wore peacock feather earrings and was the most fabulous woman I have ever known. Thank you for everything, Mom. You were simply amazing.

Thank you to my father, Hal, an entrepreneur before being an entrepreneur was cool. He was a self-made and self-taught brilliant man who created his own opportunities. He taught me that intestinal fortitude and sweat equity counted and never underestimated me.

Thank you to my Gram, Mary. I had the honor of being her next-door neighbor and namesake. She raised three children with the help of her mother, Maudie, after her husband died young, all while starting the first marching band in Lawrenceburg, Kentucky. Gram was a woman ahead of her time, and showed me that you could be patient and kick butt simultaneously.

Getting a project like a book out there seems to need a village. Even though I didn't have an entire town, I do have a community of fab folks who need thanking.

Thank you to my "big bro" cousin Greg for proofing *F2F* after the final edit. Even though the book had been proofed before, he *still* found corrections that needed to be made! You've got that eagle eye, Cuz!

Thank you to Mike Nunez, who was willing to let me use his photo in the chapter on humor. Thank you also to his gorgeous wife, Lisa, one of my early readers. Both Mike and Lisa also harassed me in a good-natured way to put a fork in this book and get it out there!

A big thank you to all of my fab early version book readers: Lisa Nunez, Lisa Broesch Weeks, Lisa Barca-Hall (aka Bubbles), Al Hencken, Teresa Ninh, and Jerry Thompson. You are all busy and successful in your own rights, but you took the time to read and give feedback on the book. You guys are the bomb!

Thanks to those who gave their impressions and suggestions on the book presentation and more during "crunch time," including Bob Kelso, Dr. Linda Walby, Dr. Julie Roseboom, Tiffany Bowen, and Linda Macdonald. Your enthusiasm for this project warms my heart.

Eddie Roseboom, the fabulously talented artist responsible for F2F's cover design, is possibly the most patient human on the planet. Eddie, the cover makes me happy every time I see it. Thank you!!!

Although I have had the benefit of many extraordinary teachers, there are a few key individuals who need thanking.

Thank you to Dr. Jane Burkhead, my Ph.D. major professor. She was a tiny but fierce woman with post-polio. In response to a disagreeable professor regarding accommodations I needed for rheumatoid, Jane related, "Sometimes those who don't like you are a good reflection on you." Words of wisdom, Jane. I've never forgotten them.

Thank you to Dr. Kurt Johnson, who also helped stick up for me against discrimination during my graduate programs. Kurt, you were always the coolest!

Thank you to Dr. Frederick Schmitt, distinguished neuropsychologist and my mentor. The education you provided me paved the way for many of my professional opportunities. You let me soak up every drop of your knowledge and tag along every chance I got!

Thank you to Dr. Jacques Caldwell, Rheumatologist. He took over my care as a 12-year-old with Juvenile Rheumatoid when there were no cures or treatments, and somehow kept me moving. I was always a person to him and not just a case. He was my first example of a doctor who truly cared and treated patients like they mattered.

· ❤ · ❤ · ❤ · ❤ · ❤ ·

I also have fun people in my life who contribute to my daily dose of happiness. Thank you to the gang, who know how to laugh, share good times, and support each other. You know who you are. You're the best!

· ❤ · ❤ · ❤ · ❤ · ❤ ·

Thank you to my big extended loving family, whom I cherish. Thinking of all of my uncles, aunts, and cousins is like a big warm hug!

· ❤ · ❤ · ❤ · ❤ · ❤ ·

And, of course, thank you to my micro-fam.

Thank you to Mickey aka Mickey Doodles, the "baby," who puts a smile on my face every day with her antics. You are always happy to run errands and do other tasks for me, which is a huge time-saver. Thank you for being so speedy and efficient and not easily distracted by bright shiny objects (like I am)! And you are great at "weighing in" whenever I need a quick opinion. Also, thank you for letting me use your tremendous double stag jump in the "Carpe Diem" photo. Your zeal for the moment has filled my heart since you were itty bitty.

Thank you also to Mickey's dog Mazie, who doubles the laughter in the house with her shenanigans. And thank you to my fabulous little marshmallow Isabella Chanel, for being a fierce and glamorous four-pound alpha.

Thank you to the "big kids" Becca and Shane. Shane, even though we're not together every day, you mean the world to me. Your sweetness and concern make everyone feel lucky to know you. And I love sharing a streak with you!

Becca, my verbal thought buddy, thank you for humoring my obsessiveness and never tiring of giving additional input, reviews, and advice. When asked your opinion on any number of topics, from wording to design, you are immediately "all in." Your creativity and warmth are inspirational.

And finally, the hugest thanks goes to Kev. You have faith in me and are my biggest fan. You always encourage me, look out for me, and love my kind of fabulous. You are my rock, and you always bring me up. You're my best and favorite fab friend. Thank you for being there, from my dissertation to seeing this book through and everything in between. You rock! I love you.

Made in the USA
Columbia, SC
23 December 2024

50531244R00191